HOME OFFICE RESEARCH STUDY NO. 91

Grievance procedures in prisons: a study of prisoners' applications and petitions

by John Ditchfield and Claire Austin

A HOME OFFICE
RESEARCH AND PLANNING UNIT
REPORT

LONDON: HER MAJESTY'S STATIONERY OFFICE

HOME OFFICE RESEARCH STUDIES

'Home Office Research Studies' comprise reports on research undertaken in the Home Office to assist in the exercise of its administrative functions, and for the information of the judicature, the services for which the Home Secretary has responsibility (direct or indirect) and the general public.

On the last pages of this report are listed titles already published in this series, in the preceding series *Studies in the Causes of Delinquency and the Treatment of Offenders,* and in the series of *Research and Planning Unit Papers.*

Her Majesty's Stationery Office

Standing order service

Placing a standing order with HMSO BOOKS enables a customer to receive other titles in this series automatically as published.

This saves time, trouble and expense of placing individual orders and avoids the problem of knowing when to do so.

For details please write to HMSO BOOKS (PC13A/1), Publications Centre, PO Box 276, London, SW8 5DT and quoting reference X25.08.07.

The standing order service also enables customers to receive automatically as published all material of their choice which additionally saves extensive catalogue research. The scope and selectivity of the service has been extended by new techniques, and there are more than 3,500 classifications to choose from. A special leaflet describing the service in detail may be obtained on request.

Foreword

Grievance procedures are the means by which prisoners may bring any requests, complaints or grievances that they have to the attention of prison staff, and thence if necessary to prison Boards of Visitors or to the Home Secretary. Such procedures are an important part of prison life, both for inmates and for those with responsibility for managing the prison system.

The Research and Planning Unit has carried out a study of these procedures in a sample of six prisons for adult male offenders. The aims of the study were to identify variations in practice between prisons and to assess the confidence which staff and inmates appeared to have in grievance procedures, in order to see what changes to policy and practice might be necessary or desirable. That study is the subject of this report.

MARY TUCK
Head of Research and Planning Unit

September 1986

Acknowledgements

We would like to thank the Governors and members of staff of the six prisons concerned in this study for their co-operation, help and interest. Thanks are also due to the Chairmen and members of their Boards of Visitors who allowed us to interview them, attend their meetings and observe them at work. Finally, we should like to acknowledge our debt to the large number of prisoners who were interviewed in this study, many of whom provided us with valuable insights into the operation of grievance procedures.

JOHN DITCHFIELD
CLAIRE AUSTIN

Contents

1 Introduction

Introduction

In prison, inmates are particularly dependent upon other people for the fulfilment of their needs and the resolution of their problems. These needs may be quite minor, for example a need for an extra letter or to have an item of property sent out of the prison, or they may take a more serious form such as a need to complain about medical treatment or make a complaint against staff. But in either case, procedures have been developed for inmates to follow with a view to their requests and grievances being properly considered.

The satisfactory operation of these procedures for dealing with inmates' requests and grievances—'grievance procedures' as they are known in prisons—plays an important role in the management and control of prisons; from this point of view a successful system is one in which prisoners can feel confident that their requests and complaints are being dealt with quickly and fairly (whether or not the outcome is satisfactory to them); an unsuccessful system can exacerbate the inevitable anxieties and tensions of prison life.

In 1983, the Home Office Research and Planning Unit undertook a study of these procedures in a sample of six prisons for adult male offenders. The aims of the study were to identify variations in practice between prisons and to assess the confidence which staff and inmates appeared to have in them, in order to see what changes to policy and practice might be necessary or desirable. That study is the subject of this report.

Current grievance procedures

In the first instance, any request or grievance by an inmate, however serious, is registered by making an 'application'. Typically, an inmate will queue up to see his wing senior or principal officer to make his application. If it is a minor problem (for example checking his eligibility for extra visits or letters, replacing inadequate or worn kit etc) then the officer may well deal with it himself. Usually, the more substantial problems are referred upwards to the next tier of the hierarchy, the 'duty governor', that is the member of the governor grades with the responsibility for taking applications on any particular day. This may be the Governor himself (the 'No 1' Governor as he is often referred to by staff and inmates), the deputy governor or one of the assistant governors.

1

Certain subject matters must be referred to the duty governor, for example applications for home leave, permission to send out photographs, permission to make a telephone call; in these cases the wing officer does not have the authority to make the decision and when the inmate makes his application at wing level it is in the nature of an administrative formality whereby he simply asks "to be put down to see the governor". Often, however, the referral of the complaint to the duty governor is as a means of appeal against a wing decision; for example, an inmate might ask the principal officer for permission to have a china cup allowed out from his stored property for his personal use, and the officer might refuse on the grounds that it could "be used as an offensive weapon". The inmate would then have the choice of either accepting this ruling or taking the matter to the duty governor in the hope of obtaining a different decision.

Thus, applications are more varied and unpredictable at duty governor level than at wing level: they include substantial matters that are best dealt with at this level, matters that must be referred to this level because of their subject matter, and matters that are in the nature of appeals against decisions made at wing level. But applications might also be referred up for other reasons: 'personal'—because the inmate does not wish to disclose a particular problem to a particular officer or assistant governor; 'litigious'—because the inmate wants to pursue the problem or complaint through all channels available; 'psychological'—because the inmate has a desire not to 'get lost in the crowd' and to get the governor to remember his face; and 'a need for reassurance'— because the inmate wants someone to listen to his problem and express interest or sympathy. Because of these and similar reasons, many of the applications referred to duty governor level concern matters that can be satisfactorily resolved at wing level (indeed, many of them are eventually referred back), but staff are usually prepared to accept this as a necessary consequence of being accessible.

As previously noted, the duty governor may not be the Governor of the prison, but his deputy or one of the assistant governors. In these circumstances if an inmate is dissatisfied with the decision that has been made, then he has the option of asking to see the 'No 1'. From the inmate's point of view, this gives him the advantage of seeing the most senior person in the prison and thus assuring himself that he has exhausted all possibilities within the internal prison hierarchy.

If an inmate is dissatisfied with the way his problem or grievance has been dealt with at duty governor level (or by the Governor), then he might consider taking his case to the Board of Visitors. (Every prison establishment has a Board of Visitors appointed by the Home Secretary. They are independent lay people who are required to be 'watchdogs' on behalf of the Home Secretary; they also carry out adjudications on prisoners who have offended against prison discipline). The inmate may ask to see the Board at an earlier stage in

2

the proceedings, but because members usually prefer the inmate to have exhausted the internal procedures first, the Board of Visitors effectively forms the next tier of grievance procedures after the duty governor.

The inmate may make his application to individual members of the Board during their inspection or 'rota' tours of the prison, to a panel of members which meets specially to hear such applications (often referred to as a 'clinic'), or to the monthly meeting of the full Board of Visitors. Practices vary from prison to prison: for example, not all prisons operate a panel system and not all Boards allow applications to be taken at their monthly meetings, so that the appropriate next stage will be specific to the prison concerned.

The inmate also has the option of submitting a written petition to the Home Secretary. Petitions are processed by staff of the Prison Department within the Home Office (either at Prison Department Headquarters or in Regional Offices, depending on subject matter) and carry the authority of the Home Secretary. Inmates can petition about any subject, but in practice many petitions are referred to the Home Office either compulsorily because it alone is empowered to deal with the matter (for example, queries about parole, queries about conviction or sentence, representations against decisions to deport etc) or because it is a long established Home Office custom to deal with that particular subject (for example permission to have photographs taken, compensation for lost or damaged property). In either case, the petition functions as a request mechanism and the role of prison staff is mostly to provide the necessary information and advice on which the Home Office can reach a decision. In other circumstances, the petition acts as an appeal mechanism whereby the inmate tries to persuade the Home Office to countermand or set aside a local decision.

Like governor's applications, the petition system can serve other, less easily defined, purposes. For example, it can act as a 'safety-valve': when inmates have had their requests refused, they can sometimes react by demanding to petition and then withdrawing it (or not even bothering to write it out) once they have 'cooled down' or thought the matter through. Similarly, staff sometimes suggest petitioning as a way of bringing a matter to a close or dealing with a particularly persistent complainant.

In practice, inmates often take their complaint to the person in whom they have most confidence even if he is not the appropriate member of staff. For example, an inmate might have a particularly good relationship with his wing officer and prefer to channel as many problems through him as possible; alternatively, he might distrust his wing officer and (where this is allowed) go straight to the duty governor without even mentioning the matter at wing level. Consequently, the flow of applications between the various tiers tends to be complex.

3

There are also certain other formal procedures which inmates can use to ventilate their grievances. Apart from petitions to Parliament or the Queen (which are rarely used in practice), they are:

(i) Application to a Visiting Officer

Under prison rules, an inmate can ask to see a Visiting Officer of the Secretary of State. Although the term Visiting Officer is not defined by the rules, its application is confined in practice to the Regional Director or his deputy and to certain senior officers from Headquarters. Visits are usually infrequent, and an inmate may have to wait several weeks or months before he can submit his application. Consequently, such requests are few.

(ii) Legal proceedings

Inmates can also institute legal proceedings to pursue their grievances. Until recently this procedure was subject to the restriction that the grievance had first to be raised internally, but in December 1983 the Divisional Court ruled (R v Governor of Wormwood Scrubs Prison ex parte Anderson) that the requirement for simultaneous ventilation was ultra vires and that prisoners had a right of access to solicitors in seeking legal advice about the institution of possible legal proceedings. This ruling was particularly significant in the context of taking proceedings against members of staff. Previously an allegation against a member of staff had first to be raised with the Governor, and under Prison Rule 47(12) this exposed the complainant to the possibility of being charged with making 'a false and malicious allegation'. It also meant that the inmate necessarily disclosed the nature of his case and the evidence available to him before any investigation took place and without benefit of legal advice. Following the Anderson case the institution of such proceedings does not involve this jeopardy. Nevertheless, the onerous nature of such proceedings means that few grievances can be dealt with this way.

(iii) Petition to the European Commission of Human Rights (ECHR)

An inmate can submit a petition to the European Commission of Human Rights without any need to petition the Secretary of State or otherwise seek permission of the prison authorities. In practice, however, the ECHR requires the inmate to have exhausted the available methods of redress before it accepts cases for consideration. It is thus very much a 'last resort' procedure and, because of the length of time it normally takes to review and decide on cases, it is also rarely used.

(iv) An approach to the Parliamentary Commissioner for Administration (PCA)

An inmate can also approach the Parliamentary Commissioner for Administration, either directly or through a Member of Parliament. If the approach is direct, then the PCA will advise the inmate to channel his complaint via an MP, either his own MP or, if he cannot be persuaded to pursue the case, through an MP prepared to do so. However, the PCA's terms of reference more or less limit him to investigating complaints which allege maladministration rather than grievances or complaints as such; as it is usually the latter which concern inmates, rather than the technical aspects of how they might have been administered, his role in grievance procedures is necessarily limited.

(v) Letter to an MP

Of the alternative procedures, the only one that is used with any degree of regularity is that of writing to an MP. Before December 1981, an inmate could write to an MP about prison treatment or prison staff only after his complaint had been investigated internally, or following receipt of the reply to a petition. After December 1981, it was only necessary for the complaint to be raised internally or by petition before the prisoner could write to an MP (ie it was no longer necessary to await the result of internal investigations or receive a reply to a petition before writing); thus, the requirement for 'prior ventilation' was replaced by a requirement only for 'simultaneous ventilation'. Normally the MP will forward the inmate's complaint to the Home Office for investigation together with any observations or recommendations he might have. The two procedures are unlikely to result in different decisions being made, but the intervention of the MP and the fact that all letters from MPs receive a Ministerial reply means that inmates (rightly or wrongly) tend to think of the procedure as being more likely to influence the Home Office's decision than petitioning alone.

Criticisms of current grievance procedures

In recent years, grievance procedures have been subject to a number of criticisms. For example, the task of Governor's applications is often delegated by the Governor to an assistant governor or the deputy governor, and in some prisons applications rarely reach the 'No 1', even in the form of appeals against decisions taken lower down. While this arrangement is consistent with the Prison Rules, it is not what a reading of the Rules might lead inmates or the public naturally to expect. Access to the Governor is important: in their report 'Justice in Prison' (Justice, 1983), the British section of the International Commission of Jurists noted 'only two authorities, the Governor and the Home Secretary, have effective powers to investigate and remedy grievances'.

The Justice report also noted that the Prison Rules do not specify the precise procedure for dealing with complaints. In an unpublished report (Lawton, 1977), it was pointed out that there were wide differences in the kind of applications dealt with by the duty governors in the two prisons examined by the study. For example, applications for authorisation of payment from private

5

cash for newspapers and radio batteries were recorded as governor applications at one prison but as wing applications at the other; similarly, requests for petition forms were dealt with by the wing principal officer at one prison but by the Governor at the other. Since two prisons could not be representative of the wide range of different establishments within the prison system, the present study provided an opportunity to present a more detailed assessment of such practices.

The powers and duties of Boards of Visitors have also been subject to criticism. Most of this criticism has been addressed to the Boards' adjudicatory role, which is outside the scope of the present study, but a certain amount has been concerned with their role in dealing with inmates' grievances and complaints. This has focused on two areas; firstly, their effectiveness in monitoring and dealing with requests and grievances; and secondly, the extent to which their adjudicatory role compromises their independence in the eyes of inmates.

For example, both the Jellicoe Committee (Martin, 1975) and the May Committee (1979) criticised the system whereby inmates made applications to visiting members of Boards during their inspection visits of prisons; they recommended instead the development of more formal procedures such as the 'clinic' system, whereby a single member or a small group of members visited the prison each week and were available at a set time for those who wanted to see them. Maguire and Vagg (1984) also expressed reservations about the Board's role in grievance procedures: first, the efforts to allow prisoners the opportunity to make applications were sometimes insufficient; second, Boards sometimes did not take up matters where it was possible for them to do so; and third, they often failed to ensure that inmates received replies to their applications. The authors recommended that members should try to make themselves more accessible to prisoners, either by introducing the 'any applications' call (where this was not already done), or by establishing—and advertising effectively—clinics. However, they felt that clinics should be additional to, rather than displace, the traditional canvassing of applications at local prisons.

However, the chief criticism of the Board has been that its two main roles—adjudicatory and supervisory—are incompatible. In this respect, both the Jellicoe Committee and the Justice Committee (Justice, 1983) recommended that they should be separated. On the other hand, Maguire and Vagg expressed certain reservations about separation as a solution to the problem. They felt that the problem arose as much from the way in which Boards actually conducted their adjudications (and the way in which they handled their supervisory role) as it did from the existence of their disciplinary function as such. They concluded that the belief that abolition of the adjudicatory function would transform prisoners' views of Boards was almost certainly false.

6

A series of judgements by the Divisional Court since 1978 has also meant that the Board's adjudicatory function has become increasingly subject to judicial review—at least where more serious offences are concerned. Partly as a result of these judgements, the Home Secretary set up a Departmental Committee in 1984 to review the Prison Disciplinary System and included in its terms of reference the requirement to consider 'the extent to which it is appropriate to use the ordinary criminal law to deal with serious misconduct by prisoners'.

The petition system has also been subject to criticism. The May Committee echoed a long-standing concern when they reported that they had 'not been impressed by the length of time taken to answer petitions'. The quality of the responses to petitions has also been criticised on the grounds that replies are often perfunctory and formal. When an inmate has put a great deal of time and effort into producing his petition, it is not difficult to see why he should find a short or 'proforma' reply irritating. In its report for 1974/75, the Select Committee on the Parliamentary Commissioner for Administration noted:

> While not wishing to add to the delay, Your Committee feel that the aver-
> age prisoner would rather wait for a reasoned reply which will show that
> proper note of the points he has raised has been taken than have a quick
> uninformative one. This does not mean that reasons necessarily have to
> be given at great length. Nor, if they have been given in reply to an earlier
> petition, do Your Committee think they need to be repeated if a prisoner
> subsequently submits a repetitive petition. (Paragraph 51, page xix.)

A more general criticism of the petition system is that it produces too many, and too many trivial, petitions. For example, in its evidence to the Education, Arts and Home Office Sub-Committee of the Expenditure Committee in 1978, the Howard League stated:

> One means of redress which has been devalued by excessive use is the
> petition to the Home Secretary: this should be an exceptional and serious
> safeguard, not a formality used thousands of times a year and the whole
> system should be examined. ('The Reduction of Pressure on the Prison
> System, Fifteenth Report of the House of Commons Expenditure
> Committee, Volume 1, paragraph 177.)

While these and similar observations led the Expenditure Committee to rec-ommend that the system of petitioning be thoroughly reviewed, the Home Office did not accept the suggestion that petitioning should be an exceptional measure: 'to a large extent the power to petition is used as a method of appealing against local decisions and the Home Secretary is not persuaded that it would be right or practicable to restrict its exercise.' ('The Reduction of Pressure on the Prison System, Observations on the Fifteenth Report of the Expenditure Committee' Cmnd 7948, 1980, HMSO, paragraph 96.) It did, however, accept the recommendation that there should be an examination of the petition system as part of a more general review of grievance procedures:

The Committee's concern that petitions may be used excessively and their suggestion that there should be an additional method of expressing grievances indicate a need to review all procedures for ventilating grievances rather than just the system of petitioning. The Secretaries of State for the Home Departments consider that such a review is desirable in principle though not of the highest priority. (Ibid, paragraph 97.)

Prison Department's concern that all grievance procedures, rather than the petition system alone should be reviewed, reflected a certain pessimism about their ability to reduce the overall level of petitioning. Efforts had been made in the past to reduce the numbers of petitions forwarded to the Home Office, but they seem to have had little effect; indeed a census conducted by the Home Office Research and Planning Unit in 1981 showed them to be running at an annual rate of approximately 12,000, compared with a rate nearer 10,000 in 1977. However, these large numbers reflect the fact noted earlier that the petition system operates as a formal request mechanism as well as an appeal mechanism against local decisions. Moreover, most of these formal request type petitions are of the 'compulsory referral' sort (ie matters concerning parole, sentence and conviction etc) while only a small proportion are of the 'customary referral' sort (ie requests to send out photographs, to change one's name, etc). Thus, even if responsibility for dealing with the latter type of petition were delegated to the local level, the reduction achieved would still be small.

It has also been argued that some reduction might be achieved if greater efforts were made to resolve complaints and grievances before they became appeal-type petitions. However, Prison Standing Orders state that 'when the matter about which a prisoner seeks to petition is a request which the Governor is able and willing to grant, the Governor should inform the prisoner of this and that a petition will not be necessary' (Standing Order 5B 4(1)), and, as will be discussed in chapter 3, it would seem that the bulk of appeal type petitions result from refusal to grant requests, rather than from inadequate or faulty consideration of requests per se. Thus, as with greater delegation, the potential for reducing the level of petitioning by improved grievance procedures is probably limited. As Prison Department stated in its written evidence to the Home Affairs Committee in 1980:

The only ways to reduce the number of petitions are those we are examining—better grievance procedures at local level and greater delegation—but the savings can only be marginal. Decisions on subjects like transfers, the Royal Prerogative of Mercy and parole cannot be delegated and many other petitions are appeals against a decision which has been made by the governor or warden. (Fourth Report from the Home Affairs Committee; The Prison Service, HC 412, Vol 1, HMSO.)

The research study

Because of these criticisms and its commitment to the Expenditure Committee to review grievance procedures, Prison Department asked the Home Office Research and Planning Unit to undertake a study of the various procedures for dealing with requests and grievances.

Previous work by the Home Office Research and Planning Unit had shown that the petitioning rate of a prison was closely associated with the kind of population catered for by that prison; for example, rates were higher in closed prisons than in open prisons, higher in mens' prisons than in womens' prisons, higher in adult establishments than in young offender establishments, and higher at dispersal prisons than at training or local prisons. It was therefore decided to limit the study to male adult sentenced prisoners in different types of closed prison, these being the sort of inmates most likely to petition and therefore most likely to make extensive use of grievance procedures.

A sample of six prisons was therefore chosen to represent the three types of closed prison concerned, comprising two locals, two training and two dispersals. With each pair an attempt was made to select two prisons that appeared to have similar population characteristics (eg in terms of the inmates' length of sentence, type of offence, age etc) but discrepant petition rates (ie one high and one low), in the expectation that such differences would reflect differences in practices for dealing with grievances, rather than different population characteristics. The population characteristics listed in Appendix A indicate that the matching of each pair was imperfect but within acceptable limits for present purposes.

The first aim of the study, the description of variations in practices, was achieved by the analysis of prison records and observations of applications made by inmates to wing staff, governors and members of Boards of Visitors. The second aim, the assessment of staff and inmate confidence in grievance procedures, was studied by interviewing staff, Board members and samples of inmates with different experiences of the petitioning system. An analysis was also made of the petition files of those inmates in the sample who had forwarded a petition to the Home Office: this was done in order to compare their own accounts of what had happened to their petitions with the actual processing that had taken place.

2 Practices in dealing with prisoners' requests and grievances

Background

The following description of practices in dealing with prisoners' requests and grievances is based partly on observational fieldwork and partly on examination of records. The fieldwork consisted of observing applications being made by inmates at the various levels of the prison hierarchy (wing officers, duty governors and Boards of Visitors), and interviewing a number of people at each of these levels.

While these observations and interviews provided suitable material for a description and comparison of practices, they did not permit adequate quantification of applications in terms of numbers, subject matter and outcome. Consequently, an analysis was made of records of applications kept by the prisons to provide the necessary quantification. At wing and duty governor levels, the period covered by the analysis was the month of November 1982. A complementary analysis of applications to the Board of Visitors and petitions to the Home Secretary was based on a three-month period (October to December 1982) because the numbers involved were much smaller at these levels than at wing or governor levels and comparisons based on one month's figures might have proved unreliable.

The use of these records involved acceptance of certain limitations. For example, at Local 2 the record of duty governors' applications rarely indicated whether the applications had been made by sentenced or remand prisoners and whether by adults or young prisoners and a considerable amount of work was necessary to establish their origin. At Dispersal 2, it was the practice on some wings for the duty governor to write directly into the wing application book rather than keep his own separate record of applications; as a result, it was not always easy to tell whether some applictions had been dealt with at wing level or governor level. Because of such difficulties, the figures given for applications in this chapter should be treated as reasonable indications of the magnitudes involved rather than as accurate enumerations.

Wing level applications

Although wing applications could be taken by basic grade, senior or principal officers, in practice they tended to be taken by the senior officer in his office on the wing. However, prisons differed in the formality of these sessions; at the local prisons they tended to be rather formal and confined to a particular period of the day (between morning unlock and breakfast), whereas at the training and dispersal prisons they were taken in a more informal, 'open door' manner, at more or less any time of the day, with clusterings after morning unlock and again before evening association.

Most formally recorded wing applications consisted of minor or routine requests which required some form of administrative record before action could be taken: for example, orders for batteries, newspapers and toiletries; requests for extra letters and extended visits; or permission to hand out authorised items on visits or to have items handed in. (Appendix B reproduces a page from the application book of B wing at one of the local prisons, which lists some 16 applications for a typical day. The 'decision' column notes the action taken which, on that day, either consisted of issuing the actual item requested—ie the special letter forms—or sending the authorising F35 form to the appropriate department of the prison for action.)

Table 1 gives the numbers of applications formally recorded in the wing application book in November 1982 for each of the six prisons, both in absolute terms and in proportion to their population.

Table 1
Formally recorded wing applications, November 1982, by prison

Applications	Local		Training		Dispersal	
	1	*2*	*1*	*2*	*1*	*2*
Number	602	765	1,216	632	732	1,212
Average number per 100 inmates	96.9	250.8	289.5	123.9	268.1	309.2

The six prisons had comparable, though not identical, recording practices at wing level. For example, requests to purchase batteries were recorded as wing applications at Training 1, but not at Training 2; newspaper orders were recorded in the wing application book at Local 2, but not at Local 1. However, the large majority of subject matters recorded at wing level were common to all six prisons.

In addition to the large number of applications dealt with formally at wing level, a considerable number were also dealt with informally (ie were not recorded). Such applications tended to be of a more general or welfare nature than the request-type applications that required a formal record. They tended to be queries about the progress of a parole review, complaints about other inmates' behaviour, disputes about entitlements etc. Such applications could be quite complicated: for example, at one training prison an inmate came into the wing office and asked the senior officer for advice about his rather involved state of affairs with the police and the courts; the inmate's problem was discussed at length and advice was given (and taken), but no record or note was made of this 'application'.

Informal applications were most common at the training and dispersal prisons, reflecting the greater informality of these regimes and their more developed state of staff/inmate relations. Far fewer informal applications occurred at the local prisons. The rapid turnover of population, the level of staff involvement in court duties and the long lock-up periods of the locals limited opportunities for dealing with inmates informally and, at the same time, increased the importance of maintaining a high level of documentation.

However, such differences in the six prisons' informal application rates could not account for the differences in their formal application rates. It has already been noted that informal applications were more common at the training and dispersal prisons than at the local prisons. Additionally, however, observation showed them to be more common at Training 1 than at Training 2 and more common at Local 2 than at Local 1. Thus, aggregating informal application rates with formal application rates would, if anything, increase the differences noted in Table 1.

Thus, the variation in recorded wing application rates between the six prisons could not be accounted for by differences in recording practices or the proportion of informal applications. At the same time, the differences in application rates were much greater than would be expected by chance ($p<.001$), indicating a need to examine which other factors (eg difference in regime or population characteristics) might account for these statistically significant differences. Some factors which might have influenced wing application rates are examined below.

Local prisons

Table 1 shows Local 1 to have the lowest rate of wing applications of the six prisons. One of the most notable features of Local 1 was a tradition of firm inmate discipline. A Prison Inspectorate Report had noted the unusual degree of confidence and assertiveness amongst staff and attributed this to their seniority and to the fact that many of them had spent their entire service at that prison. Perhaps as a result of this tradition, there was a tendency on the part of uniformed staff to try and deal with as many applications as possible themselves; "we try not to give the assistant governors anything" was one senior officer's comment; another said "inmates at (Local 1) just never complain formally: the food here is repetitive and monotonous, yet inmates never complain about it". It is worth noting in this respect that none of the governor grades interviewed thought that wing staff referred too many applications to them.

Local 2 had a much higher rate of wing applications (Table 1). At Local 2 it was also the uniformed staff's policy to ask inmates why they wanted to see the Governor, partly for information and partly to see whether the problem could be resolved without troubling him. However, if the inmate insisted on seeing the Governor, or refused to reveal the reason why he wanted to see him, the case would be readily referred up; as one senior officer said "as I understand it, the inmate has a right to see the Governor, so even if he does not tell me what it is about, I put him down". As a result, grievance procedures at Local 2 may have reflected the Governor's policy of allowing inmates a reasonable degree of latitude in expressing their grievances, the Governor himself stating "I believe the inmate has an inherent right to see the 'No 1', so often I deal with things that could be done by the wings. The Governor must not get isolated and I can keep a finger on the pulse of the prison by dealing with applications".

Training prisons

As already mentioned, access to wing staff at the two training prisons was on a more informal 'open-door' basis than at the local prisons. Inmates could see the wing senior officer (and/or the wing principal officer) at more or less any time they were available. Nevertheless, there was still a clustering of applications at morning unlock and before evening association, the pattern being more pronounced at Training 2 than at Training 1. At Training 1 the senior officers were particularly 'exposed' and busy: one senior officer said "it's more demanding to work the type of informal application system we have here (ie compared with locals), it's particularly draining on the senior officer, there's a barrage of queries the whole day".

Pressure on the senior officers seemed to be somewhat less at Training 2, probably reflecting the co-operative nature of the inmates and possibly the 'filtering' effect of its 'SWIP' (Social Work in Prisons) scheme. Under this scheme, some of the basic grade staff were designated as 'group' officers with special concern for the welfare of about 12–14 men under their supervision. They were supposed to be the first point of contact for any of their inmates who had a request or problem of a welfare nature. The officer might, for example, make a telephone call to enquire why the inmate's wife, mother, etc, had not appeared at a visit, or enquire about the health of a sick relative, or contact the inmate's probation officer. Being informal, and largely concerned with welfare matters, no formal record of such contacts were kept. Applications or requests that required some form of written authority or record went, as normal, to the wing senior officer to deal with.

The filtering effect of the SWIP scheme is difficult to assess; for while it may have filtered out some of the more welfare-type applications at landing level, these would not normally have gone to the senior officer anyway, being directed straight to the welfare department instead. It thus seems likely that the impact of SWIP was more on the workload of the prison's probation staff rather than grievance procedures per se.

Dispersal prisons

Like staff at the training prisons, wing staff at the dispersals were usually available on an informal 'open-door' basis. However, their role was less pronounced than at the training prisons, probably reflecting the general preference of long term and life sentence inmates to deal with the more senior levels of prison staff. Theere was a feeling among assistant governors at Dispersal 2 that perhaps too many applications were referred up from wing level, resulting from Dispersal 2's rather complex procedures, rather than from any shortcomings on the part of wing staff. At Dispersal 1 there was also a feeling that too many applications were referred to duty governor level: one assistant governor said "in the dispersal system it's difficult to give uniformed staff discretion because they just say 'yes'...", implying that inmates at dispersals were more difficult for uniformed staff to refuse than they were at other prisons.

Wing managers' applications

At two of the prisons (Training 1 and Dispersal 2) there was an intermediate level of referral between the senior officer and the duty governor—'wing managers'. This tier consisted of the wing principal officer and the wing assistant governor who shared an office on the wing and were available to the inmates on an informal basis, by way of the 'open-door' policy. As such, the concept of wing manager straddled the uniform and governor grades and demanded a degree of co-operation between the two. Their impact on grievance procedures seemed to be rather limited. Certainly, very few applications were recorded at this level in either prison and, because the arrangement was limited to only two of the prisons, it was excluded from the numerical comparisons.

Governors' and duty governors' applications

Duty governor applications were the most important forum within the prison for the resolution of requests and complaints. As previously noted, the duty governor can be an assistant governor, the deputy governor or the 'No 1' Governor himself. At Local 1, Training 2 and Dispersal 2, the duty governor was usually an assistant governor, whereas at Local 2, Training 2 and Dispersal 1, he was usually the Governor.

Duty governors' applications were taken on the same daily basis as wing applications, except at Training 1, where they were also taken on Saturday mornings, but at a later time—usually mid to late morning. When considering applications, governors usually had a member of staff present to brief them as necessary, and the inmate's file to consult. If any action was required, the authorising F35 form would be sent to the appropriate department or officer at the prison.

15

Table 2
Applications made to duty governors in November 1982, by number and per hundred inmates

Applications	Local		Training		Dispersal	
	1	2	1	2	1	2
Number	41	108	295	68	180	121
Average number per 100 inmates	6.6	35.4	70.2	13.3	65.9	30.9

Table 2 shows the workload of applications at duty governor levels in the six prisons in November 1982. The differences in application rates at duty governor levels were much greater than would be expected by chance ($p<.001$). The pattern of variation was generally similar to the pattern of variation for wing applications and equally could not be explained in terms of the different prison concerned: the lowest rates again were at Training 2 and Local 1.

Table 3 presents the applications in terms of their subject matter. The most common subjects were visits, local privileges, employment and wages, transfer, private cash, property and diet; together they accounted for over half of governors' applications. However, considerable variations are evident in the incidence of different subject matters between prisons. At the two local prisons there was a large number of applications about allocations and transfers, which reflected inmates' anxieties at these prisons about their present and future location; at the dispersal prisons there was a large number of applications about local privileges, reflecting these inmates' greater concern about the quality of their imprisonment. Some types of applications were more or less specific to the prison concerned; for example, the large number of applications about private cash at Training 1 reflected a local administrative feature which enabled its inmates to transfer a certain amount of money from their private cash to their canteen fund. However, the analysis of subject matter did not indicate why the six prisons should have such different rates of applications to governors. Other factors which might account for the different rates are considered below.

Local prisons

At Local 1, most applications were taken by the wing's own assistant governor with the relevant principal officer present to brief him. It was not the practice at Local 1 to allow inmates to pursue their applications to the Governor too readily; indeed he was not really accessible for this purpose. The assistant governors, although wing based, were also somewhat inaccessible, partly because their duties took them away from the wing for so much of the day, and partly because, as previously noted, it was the tradition at the prison for uniformed staff to deal with as many applications as possible themselves.

Table 3

Applications made to the duty governor, by subject matter and by prison, November 1982

Subject Matter	Local		Training		Dispersal		Total	
	1	2	1	2	1	2	Number	Per cent
Visits	6	10	26	12	11	16	81	10.0
Local privileges, eg hobbies and clothing regulations	2	8	16	5	28	14	73	9.0
Employment/Wages	2	14	32	4	7	6	65	8.0
Transfer and allocation to other prisons	11	21	2	6	19	1	60	7.4
Inmates' private cash	—	1	37	2	3	8	51	6.3
Inmates' property	—	2	22	3	5	18	50	6.2
Diet	3	1	13	—	9	14	40	4.9
Petitions, eg replies and progress queries	2	7	10	3	7	—	29	3.6
Correspondence, eg extra letters and postage	2	4	6	1	10	5	28	3.4
Medical	1	3	12	3	5	3	27	3.3
Temporary release, eg day's parole for funeral attendance	—	—	18	3	4	—	25	3.1
Local treatment and conditions, eg lack of barber	—	1	9	1	7	3	21	2.6
Education, eg requests to join courses	2	—	6	—	8	—	16	2.0
Short home leave, eg pre-parole leave	1	1	8	1	3	1	14	1.7
Prison issued kit	—	1	7	1	3	—	13	1.6
Phone calls	—	1	4	1	1	5	12	1.5
Permission to hand out/hand in articles on a visit	—	—	5	1	1	4	11	1.4
Rule 43, ie segregation for self-protection	1	9	—	—	—	—	10	1.2
Legal, eg appeals against conviction and sentence	—	1	3	3	1	2	10	1.2
Personal matters, (often not specified)	—	—	5	—	2	2	9	1.1
Request to see the Board of Visitors	1	1	4	—	—	3	9	1.1
Production at court	—	2	3	3	1	—	9	1.1
Parole	—	1	4	1	1	1	8	1.0
Subject matter not specified	2	3	2	—	20	2	29	3.6
Misc (any subject matter accounting for less than 1% of the sample)	5	16	41	14	24	13	113	13.9
Total	41	108	295	68	180	121	813	100.0

At Local 2, applications were taken by the Governor himself or, if he were unavailable, by his deputy or one of the assistant governors. Unlike Local 1, the assistant governors were not located on the wings and did not normally take applications. In most cases the Governor would be briefed beforehand by the chief officer's clerk and the chief officer himself would also be present. As previously noted, uniformed staff at Local 2 had a policy of trying to establish the reasons why inmates wanted to see the Governor, although it was not clear how far this policy was observed in practice; certainly there was no equivalent of Local 1's staff practice of shielding the Governor and assistant governors.

Training prisons

At Training 1, duty governor's applications were taken by the Governor or, if he were unavailable, by the deputy governor. The applications were taken on the wings during the Governor's morning tour of the prison, with the relevant wing principal officer or assistant governor present to brief him. The journeys through the prison produced a considerable amount of inmate/Governor contact, the Governor frequently stopping to talk with individual prisoners and even, on occasion, taking informal applications from them. This system of the morning tour enabled the Governor to be accessible to inmates on a daily basis and to keep in close touch with the day-to-day life of the prison. Indeed, of the six prisons in the sample, Training 1 had by far the most accessible Governor.

At Training 2, the duty governor was one of two assistant governors who each had responsibility for two of the prison's four 'houses' or wings. The chief officer was usually present to brief him. Unlike Training 1, the Governor never took morning applications, although occasionally a problem might be referred up to him. To some extent, the assistant governor was shielded by the wing senior officer and by Training 2's SWIP system of encouraging basic grade officers to deal with men's welfare problems.

Although the impact of shielding is difficult to assess, it may be significant that in comparison with Training 1, applications at Training 2 tended to be dealt with a 'grade down'. However, as the Governor at Training 1 pointed out, while many of the applications brought to his attention could have been dealt with lower down, delegation in this respect was not an over-riding consideration: the morning tour and taking morning applications were part of a conscious policy of keeping in touch with staff and inmates on a daily basis and maintaining accessibility.

Dispersal prisons

In theory, duty governor's applications at Dispersal 1 could be taken either by the Governor, the deputy governor, a governor IV or one of the two assistant governors. In practice, the Governor or deputy governor took applications from the main wings and the governor IV took applications from the hospital. The Governor at Dispersal 1 was not shielded by staff from inmates' applications although he was not as accessible and visible as the Governor at Training 1.

At Dispersal 2, governor's applications used to be taken either by the governor IV or by one of the wing assistant governors. The chief officers' clerk was usually present to brief him. The use of wing assistant governors for duty governor's applications could sometimes pose problems: an inmate could go to his wing assistant governor with a request or problem, be dissatisfied with the response and put down for governor's applications—only to find the same assistant governor acting as duty governor that particular morning. The assistant governor would find it difficult to do other than go through the motions of dealing with the problem afresh, or the inmate would have to come back another day. This had been one of the problems which had motivated a review of grievance procedures at Dispersal 2.

Applications to the Governor himself at Dispersal 2 were not encouraged and considerable efforts were made to persuade the inmate to have his problems dealt with by the duty governor. Consequently, a degree of perseverance was required if an inmate wished to see the Governor and 'No 1 inaccessibility' was a frequent complaint. Following a local review of procedures the Governor now takes applications each morning.

Boards of Visitors' applications

Boards of Visitors deal with two types of applications—general applications concerning complaints and grievances, and applications for the restoration of lost remission, ie remission forfeited by inmates as a punishment by the Board in its adjudicatory role. General applications may be made by inmates to individual members of the Board during their inspection or rota visit of the prison, or to the full Board. An application to be heard by the Board as such may be heard by a quorum of three members and some Boards arrange this sitting as a 'clinic' between monthly meetings of the Board. (However, the study found that applicants sometimes found it difficult to accept that a three man quorum could technically act as a full Board and insisted on their right of access to a 'full Board'. Confusion also existed among both inmates and Board members as to whether the inmate's right of access was to the full Board or simply to a member of the Board.) Practices varied depending on which of these options were available in each prison. Table 4 shows that most applications were dealt with during rota visits at Local 1, Training 2 and Dispersal 1, by panels at Training 1 and Dispersal 2, and by the monthly Board meeting at Local 2.

In general, applications for the restoration of lost remission were considered by the full Board at its monthly meeting, either by direct application (as at Local 2), or in the form of recommendations submitted by special panels of members who interviewed and assessed the inmates concerned. The latter system was used at Training 1, Dispersal 1 and Dispersal 2. However, at Training 2, the panel both heard and decided the outcome of the application. At Local 1 there were no fixed procedures for hearing these applications; Board Members tended to deal with them when they came to prison to take adjudications.

Table 4

General applications and applications for the restoration of lost remission made to Boards of Visitors, October to December 1982

Type of Application	Local		Training		Dispersal		Total
	1	2	1	2	1	2	
General applications during rota visits	42	1	8	7	41	5	104
General applications to panels or clinics	—	—	17	—	16	43	76
General applications to monthly meetings	3	6	—	—	—	—	9
Sub total	45	7	25	7	57	48	189
Applications for restoration of lost remission	2	—	6	3	11	9	31
Total	47	7	31	10	68	57	220
Total per 100 inmates over 3 months	7.6	2.3	7.4	2.0	24.9	14.5	

Table 5 shows the subject matter of applications made to the Boards of Visitors at the six prisons for the three-month period October to December 1982. The Boards considered 220 applications during this period. The most common subjects were restoration of lost remission, local treatment, wages and employment, diet, transfers, local privileges and adjudication awards. Together they accounted for over half of the applications made. The table shows there was some inter-prison variation where certain subject matters were concerned: for example, Dispersal 1 accounted for over half the applications about local treatment, while at Dispersal 2 (and to a lesser extent at Training 1) there was a noticeable number of applications about 'diet' which reflected known catering difficulties at those two prisons.

Of the 31 applications for restoration of lost remission, 23 were granted. In general, the main criterion for restoration of remission was some evidence of a change of attitude on the part of the inmate. The amount restored ranged from five to fifty days and, in those instances where data were available, closely followed the recommendations of the prison staff.

Table 5

Applications made to the Board of Visitors, by subject matter and by prison, October to December 1982

Subject Matter	Local		Training		Dispersal		Total	
	1	2	1	2	1	2	Number	Per cent
Restoration of lost remission	2	—	6	3	11	9	31	14.1
Local treatment and conditions, eg lack of barber	5	—	3	—	13	3	24	10.9
Employment/Wages	2	1	2	1	9	5	20	9.1
Diet	—	2	2	—	2	9	15	6.8
Transfer and allocation to other prisons	3	—	2	—	5	2	12	5.5
Adjudication award	2	2	—	1	5	—	10	4.5
Medical	2	—	1	—	1	5	9	4.1
Local privileges, eg hobbies, clothing regulations	3	—	1	—	1	5	10	4.5
Inmates' property	1	1	—	—	3	2	7	3.2
Petitions, eg replies and progress queries	1	—	2	—	3	1	7	3.2
Legal, eg appeals against conviction and sentence	1	—	—	—	1	5	7	3.2
Visits	1	1	1	2	—	—	5	2.3
Inmates' private cash	2	—	—	1	—	2	5	2.3
Categorisation	1	—	4	—	—	—	5	2.3
Parole	—	—	2	1	1	1	5	2.3
Rule 43, ie segregation for self protection	—	—	—	—	—	2	2	0.9
Canteen, ie the local facility for the purchase of goods	1	—	—	—	2	—	3	1.4
Prison issued kit	—	—	2	—	1	—	3	1.4
Correspondence, eg extra letters and postage	2	—	—	—	2	—	4	1.8
Subject matter not specified	9	—	—	—	—	2	11	5.0
Misc (any subject accounting for less than 1% of the sample)	9	—	3	1	8	4	25	11.4
Total	47	7	31	10	68	57	220	100.0

21

Local prisons

At both local prisons, inmates could make general applications to Board members during their weekly rota visits (to individual members at Local 1 and to pairs of members at Local 2). Applications could also be made at each prison to the full Board meeting. Despite the similarities in practices between Local 1 and Local 2, considerably greater use was made of the Board at Local 1 than at Local 2. The reasons for this are not clear, but two considerations may have been relevant. Firstly, the 'Local 1 tradition' of discipline and control may have made applications to the Board attractive as an alternative avenue of complaint whereas, at Local 2, the policy of Governor accessibility encouraged far more applications to be dealt with at Governor level and reduced the need for use of the Board. Secondly, the Board may have been more visible at Local 1. Altogether, about one half of the respondents at Local 2 were either unclear about who Board members were or about its role in grievance procedures. To some extent, this ignorance may have reflected the comparative youth of Local 2's population and its high proportion of inmates serving their first sentence. There was also a high proportion of first sentence offenders at Local 1 but, nevertheless, fewer inmates expressed ignorance about the Board's role in grievance procedures (perhaps partly because of more frequent usage by inmates).

Training prisons

Procedural arrangements for applications to the Board of Visitors at the two training prisons were similar. Inmates could make general applications to individual Board members during inspection visits (on a fortnightly basis at Training 1 and weekly at Training 2). At Training 1, applications were also considered by a three-member Board panel which met fortnightly. Training 2 arrangements were noteworthy in that Board members (being unaccompanied on visits) could hear applications in private. They would also attempt to deal with them on the same day, the member making enquiries and returning to the inmate with an answer or advice.

Inmate usage of the Board nevertheless was much less at Training 2, possibly for the following reasons. Firstly, the type of inmate catered for by Training 2 was very co-operative and usually concerned not to endanger parole prospects by 'rocking the boat'; asking to see the Board of Visitors might be interpreted as doing just that. Secondly, there appeared to be a problem of visibility at Training 2; as one inmate said "in this prison you don't know who are visiting magistrates (ie Board member)... they should tell you when the Board is here".

Dispersal prisons

At Dispersal 1, inmates could make general applications to individual members on their weekly rota visits or to a three-member monthly quorum. At

Dispersal 2, general applications were heard by a panel (of usually two members) which met weekly. At both dispersal prisons, there was a full Board meeting each month at which all applications received that month were discussed.

The Boards were used much more at these prisons than at either the local or training prisons (see Table 4). The reasons for this are not clear. However, the relative stability of the population at the dispersals meant that they avoided the problems of recognition and unfamiliarity with the Board's role characteristic of the locals; at the same time, the demanding and assertive nature of their inmates meant that they had inmate populations prepared to make full use of their facilities.

The petition system

Petition forms could be obtained from either wing staff or governor grades although in most cases it appeared to be the wing senior or principal officers who provided them. In some cases, certain members of staff or other inmates might help the petitioner to write his petition. Once completed, the form would be handed back to staff who would write an accompanying note or report before its despatch to the Home Office; at the locals this was completed by the assistant governors, at Training 1 by the wing managers, at Training 2 by one of the wing assistant governors, at Dispersal 1 by the wing principal officer and at Dispersal 2 by the wing managers or the governor IV. Depending on the subject matter of the petition, additional reports would be included from relevant prison staff specialists such as the senior medical officer, catering officer, or a member of the welfare staff.

Issued petition forms were often not sent forward because inmates had lost them, destroyed them or had not even bothered to fill them in. Once an inmate had completed and handed in a petition, then he usually would have to make an application to withdraw it and the petition register would be noted to that effect.

Table 6 shows the number of petitions which were forwarded, withdrawn at the inmate's own request, or not returned during the three-month period October to December 1982. The differences between the prisons in terms of numbers per inmate were much larger than would have been expected by chance ($p<.001$). Table 6 also shows that the difference in rates could not be explained by reference to the different types of prison concerned; Training 2 had a lower petition rate than either of the local prisons, yet the rate for Training 1 was little different from the rates for the dispersal prisons. As in the case of formally recorded wing applications and applications to governors (Tables 1 and 2), the lowest rates occurred at Local 1 and Training 2.

Table 6
The number of petitions at the six prisons which were forwarded, withdrawn at inmate's request or not returned, October to December 1982

Status of petition	Local		Training		Dispersal	
	1	*2*	*1*	*2*	*1*	*2*
Forwarded	42	43	89	24	66	68
Withdrawn at inmate's own request	7	13	4	2	11	8
Not returned	1	3	19	6	14	11
Total issued	50	59	112	32	91	87
Average number forwarded per 100 inmates over 3 months	6.8	14.1	21.2	4.7	24.2	17.3
Average number withdrawn or not returned per 100 inmates over 3 months	1.3	5.2	5.5	1.6	9.2	4.8

Table 7 shows the subject matter of the petitions forwarded to the Home Office, by prison. The most common subjects were transfer and allocation requests, parole, queries about employment/wages and medical problems; together these accounted for about one half of the total sample of petitions. The only clear inter-prison differences were the large proportion of petitions concerning allocations and transfers at the two local prisons (62% and 60%) and the large proportion concerning parole at the training prisons (30% and 25%). The pattern at dispersals was less clear, and seemed to be characterised, if at all, by problems specific to the prison rather than the population; for example the high level of transfers at Dispersal 1 reflected the visiting difficulties caused by its location.

Analysis of subject matter provided few clues as to why the six prisons had such different petition rates. In particular, it failed to indicate why each pair of local and training prisons should have such different rates when their inmates appeared to share common concerns—for example, allocation and transfer at the locals and parole at the training prisons. However, some differences in their practices and attitudes towards petitioning which might have contributed to different rates, are considered below.

Local prisons

Fieldwork offered few clues as to why Local 1 had a significantly lower petition rate than Local 2. Procedures at both prisons were broadly similar (petition forms being issued by wing staff and then processed by assistant governors) and inmates appeared to experience few difficulties when they actually applied to petition. However, it is just possible that Local 1's tradition of discipline and control meant that the same sort of grievances were not always pursued (or even initiated) with the same vigour as at Local 2.

Table 7
Petitions forwarded, by subject matter and by prison, October to December 1982

Subject Matter	Local		Training		Dispersal		Total	
	1	2	1	2	1	2	Number	Per cent
Transfer and allocation to other prisons	26	26	3	5	17	6	83	24.9
Parole	1	1	27	6	4	9	48	14.4
Employment/Wages	—	1	14	1	6	6	28	8.4
Medical	5	—	3	1	3	6	18	5.4
Request to have photos sent out	—	—	6	—	—	10	16	4.8
Production at court	2	2	1	3	3	3	14	4.2
Compensation for property	2	1	2	2	1	3	11	3.3
Calculation of sentence	1	2	3	—	1	1	8	2.4
Petitions, eg replies and progress queries	—	—	5	1	—	2	8	2.4
Visits	—	1	—	—	4	1	7	2.1
Diet	—	3	1	—	2	1	7	2.1
Adjudication awards	1	—	1	—	3	1	6	1.8
Legal, eg appeals against conviction and sentence	—	—	1	—	—	5	6	1.8
Restoration of lost remission	1	—	4	—	—	—	5	1.5
Temporary release, eg days parole for funeral attendance	—	—	2	1	—	1	4	1.2
Multiple, ie more than one subject	—	—	3	1	—	—	4	1.2
Subject matter not specified	—	5	2	1	21	3	32	9.6
Misc (any subject matter accounting for less than 1% of the sample)	2	1	11	2	4	9	29	8.7
Total	42	43	89	24	69	67	334	100.0

Training prisons

At Training 1, governor grades appeared to share a firm view that petitioning was a basic right of the inmate and he was not to be discouraged from using this facility. An assistant governor said "there is a powerful case for having the ability to contact the outside... we say we don't mind". In accord with this spirit, Training 1 did not observe the '28 day rule' which governs the issue of petitions. Under this rule an inmate cannot petition the Home Office if he already has a petition outstanding, unless a month has elapsed since the previous petition was submitted or the Governor considers that an exception should be made. There are certain exceptions to this rule; for example, petitions about conviction and sentence, parole, deportation or interference with correspondence.

At Training 2 (on the other hand), staff attitudes were more ambivalent. A large proportion of inmates were very much concerned with their chances of parole and this created a climate in which they tended to see their best interests to be that of co-operating with staff, or at least of keeping a low profile. This militated against making too many complaints or unmerited petitions. At the same time, the anxiety created by parole, and the disappointment of a refusal, resulted in a high level of petitions concerning parole. The attitude of staff was, if anything, sympathetic to this kind of petition: "I would never advise not to petition about a 'knock back' (parole refusal). If I feel it was a bad decision we discuss it and sometimes I help with the phrasing". Thus inmates and staff alike appeared to make an unstated distinction between petitions about parole (a legitimate right and 'nothing to do with us') and other sorts of petitions (possibly indicative of 'trouble making').

Dispersal prisons

Like Training 1, neither dispersal prison observed the '28 day rule' governing the issue of petitions. Likewise, both prisons adopted an attitude of neutrality towards petitioning. As one assistant governor said "we adopt a neutral stance towards grievances and petitions, we don't obstruct and we don't encourage it, we give advice"; another said "we don't encourage petitions as they encourage paperwork, if he (the inmate) insists however, he can... we don't mind how many go out, but we don't encourage it".

The rather higher petitioning rate of Dispersal 1 probably reflected its geographical isolation which meant that a large proportion of petitions were concerned with transfers and related problems.

Summary

Table 8 summarises the monthly rate of applications at each level of grievance procedure in each of the six prisons.

Table 8
The monthly rate of applications per 100 inmates considered by wing staff, duty governors, Boards of Visitors or by petition at each of the six prisons

Level of application	Local		Training		Dispersal	
	1	2	1	2	1	2
Recorded wing applications*	96.9	250.8	289.5	123.9	268.1	309.2
Applications considered by duty governor*	6.6	35.4	70.2	13.3	65.9	30.9
Applications considered by the Board of Visitors**	2.5	0.8	2.5	0.7	8.3	4.8
Petitions forwarded**	2.3	4.7	7.1	1.6	8.1	5.8

*November 1984   **Figures are monthly averages for the three-month period October—December 1982

A number of interesting comparisons could be made from Table 8. However, for present purposes it is sufficient to note that the six prisons, in general, tended to have consistently high or consistently low application rates at all levels of grievance procedure, rather than high rates at some and low at others. This uniformity in the ranking of the six prisons was statistically significant (coefficient of concordance 0.69, $F = 6.5$, $p < .01$). For example, Local 1 and Training 2 had the lowest recorded wing application rates, the lowest duty governor application rates, and the lowest petition rates of the six prisons— Training 2 also had the lowest rate of applications to the Board of Visitors. Thus, the different levels of grievance procedure did not seem to act as filters for each other. This strongly implied that differences in management practices were fairly unimportant in influencing application rates. By the same token, it suggested the hypothesis that the observed differences between the prisons had either to be explained in terms of differences between their regimes (ie in terms of general policies and attitudes on the part of staff which affected application rates at all levels of grievance procedure), or in terms of the characteristics of their populations (which influenced both the need and inclination of their inmates to make use of grievance procedures), or by some combination of both.

Where the two local prisons are concerned, regime seems to have been the more important factor in accounting for the differences in their application rates. For example, both prisons had inmate populations with similar characteristics of offence and sentence (see Appendix A) and both populations were preoccupied with problems of transfer and allocation. Yet their usage of grievance procedures was very different. Local 2 had much higher application and petition rates than Local 1 (with the exception of the Board of Visitors) and it is difficult to account for this except possibly in terms of Local 1's formal regime on the one hand, and Local 2's comparatively liberal and accessible regime on the other hand. The exception—the Board of Visitors—is interesting in this respect, as the greater use of this facility at Local 1 may have

27

been the consequence of the comparative inaccessibility of internal procedures at that prison.

Where the training prisons are concerned, differences between both their regimes and the characteristics of their inmate populations seem to have been important in explaining their different application rates. For example, Training 1 encouraged the reasonably free expression of requests and grievances at all levels of procedure and was characterised by having the most accessible Governor of the six prisons. While these factors may have resulted in the expression of some requests and grievances that would not otherwise have normally entered the system, they seem, in themselves, unlikely to have accounted for the prison's high application and petition rates. These seem likely to have also reflected the demanding and assertive nature of its inmates who were prepared to make full use of the facilities available to them. The Inspectorate's report had noted that 'but for the absence of Category A prisoners, the characteristics of the inmate population of Training 1 are very similar to those of the population of a dispersal prison.' Moreover, a significant number of inmates had also served the earlier part of their sentence at dispersal prisons. On the other hand, Training 2 was characterised by a rather more formal regime which tended to discourage inmates from taking complaints and grievances to governor level. However, this factor alone seems unlikely to have accounted for its low rate of applications to the Board of Visitors and its low rate of petitions. In addition, its wing applications rate was also very low and, as noted earlier, this is considered unlikely to have been the result of the prison's SWIP scheme, which mostly affected the welfare workload. Thus, even taken together, the regime and SWIP factors seem unlikely to have accounted for the low rates recorded. Instead, they seem more likely to have been a reflection of the relatively co-operative type of inmate selected for Training 2, who was an inmate usually approaching the middle or end of his sentence and who had good chances of parole. Such inmates were, rightly or wrongly, unwilling to be thought of as troublesome and preferred to keep a low profile.

The differences between the two dispersal prisons are more difficult to explain. Their populations had apparently similar characteristics and both groups were prepared to make full use of the procedures available to them. This was particularly noticeable with respect to the Board of Visitors, inmates at both prisons making greater use of this facility than was the case at either the local or training prisons. The differences in the other application rates (which were small in comparison to the other two pairs of prisons) were probably a result of slight differences in their procedural arrangements and the location of Dispersal 1. The greater accessibility of the duty governor at Dispersal 1 probably encouraged the relatively high rate of applications at this level, whilst its geographical isolation produced a large number of petitions concerning transfer.

3 Confidence in grievance procedures

Introduction

This chapter is concerned with the second aim of the study—an assessment of the extent to which staff and inmates had confidence in current grievance procedures. Unlike the procedures themselves, confidence is difficult to observe or quantify; it is a subjective feeling that can only be reported by the subject or inferred by the observer. Moreover, within the context of prison life and its inevitable 'us and them' structure, these feelings are likely to be more than ordinarily subjective. They are also likely to be dependent on the location of the subject within the system. For example, inmates' perspectives will almost certainly be different from those of staff and, at the same time, the perspectives of the different groups which comprise the staff side (discipline staff and governor grades) are likely to differ from those of an independent, non-staff, non-inmate body such as the Board of Visitors.

The study was therefore designed to include the views of all groups, although the main emphasis was given to the views and attitudes of inmates. Structured interviews were held with 29 wing officers at senior and principal level (with recent experiences of dealing with applications), 23 members of governor grades (including the six Governors of the prisons), 24 member of Boards of Visitors and 257 inmates. The latter sample consisted of 202 inmates who had had recent experience of submitting or withdrawing petitions and 55 inmates with little or no such experience. The staff samples were perhaps smaller than would have been ideal (particularly for making inter-prison comparisons), but it should be borne in mind that the views obtained were supplemented by a considerable amount of informal discussion and contact during the course of fieldwork. The interview schedules were designed to be comprehensive and subjects were not discouraged from taking a discursive approach if they wished.

The results of the interviews are explored below. They are presented in terms of the group concerned—staff, Board members, inmates etc—adopted because the different groups were more familiar with certain aspects of grievance procedures than others and because it facilitated inter-prison comparisons.

Uniformed staff's views on grievance procedures

Although uniformed staff played an extensive role in dealing with inmates' applications, it was, as noted previously, largely one of dealing with the more routine requests and queries; substantive requests and grievances were normally referred to governor grades to deal with. Nevertheless, there was always a certain degree of overlap in this respect and the involvement of wing staff in grievance procedures varied from prison to prison. Consequently, a number of staff at each of the six prisons were asked a series of questions which tried to assess their attitudes to, and confidence in, procedures at wing level for dealing with inmates' applications. They were asked whether they considered applications to be an important part of their job and whether the procedures could be improved, particularly in respect of staff continuity and training and the greater involvement of landing officers.

Local prisons

Seven uniformed staff were interviewed at the two local prisons. They all rated the taking of applications as an important part of their duties. Most officers felt that greater staff continuity for applications work would necessitate missing job 'perks' of escorts and courts duties and was not justified in view of the largely routine nature of the work. There was little support for either devolution or training. In general, staff at the two local prisons appeared to consider grievance procedures at wing level largely satisfactory.

Training prisons

The taking of applications was also seen as an important part of the uniformed staff's work at the two training prisons, all 14 of the officers interviewed considering it to be important. At Training 1, some members of the sample emphasised that the senior officer had a taxing job in this respect: 'it takes a lot of time, you are dealing with a continual stream (of requests); prisoners are running about all day, you are available to them 14 hours a day and even at lunch time it's not a total lock up situation. At [another prison] you and the prisoner knew where you stood, here familiarity breeds contempt—there's a constant battle of wits here, but in a way there's more job satisfaction here'. One or two officers at Training 2 stressed the control and management aspects of the job: "next to security, it's the most important part of the job; it gives an insight into them as people and how they feel and helps to make for a quiet establishment". In general, staff at the training prisons felt that wing application procedures worked fairly well. However, there was more variety in their opinions about devolution of responsibility and staff continuity. Some felt that basic grade officers could take more responsibility but others felt that it would conflict with their control function. Officers pointed out that basic grade staff at training prisons had more responsibility than at most prisons but felt that problems of hierarchy and bureaucracy made its further extension

30

problematic. Several officers mentioned their belief that there should be more continuity in wing staff.

Dispersal prisons

Fourteen officers were interviewed at the two dispersal prisons. Dealing with applications was considered to be an important part of the senior officer's duties, particularly at Dispersal 2. This was largely because of its management and control functions. As one officer said: "it helps to keep your finger on the pulse of the wing, it's a good early warning system". As at the local and training prisons, it was clear that some officers derived considerable job satisfaction from dealing with applications.

At both prisons there was general agreement that it would be difficult to give basic grade officers a greater role in dealing with applications, partly for physical reasons (lack of suitable accommodation) and partly because inmates would 'still ignore a blue-collar, whatever his responsibilities'. Similarly, officers saw little point in the provision of special training for dealing with applications, most of them thinking it was best learnt by doing the job itself and also because 'each grade is the training grade for the grade above'. There was, however, a firm belief that there should be more continuity in the personnel dealing with applications. This was considered particularly important at Dispersal 2, all of the officers interviewed emphasising the point.

Governors' views on grievance procedures

Governors' applications

The sample of 23 governors (including the Governors of the six prisons in the sample) were asked whether there were any changes they would like to see made to grievance procedures in their prisons. Few changes were suggested and in general governors seemed fairly satisfied with their own internal procedures for dealing with inmates' requests and grievances. The problems they mentioned tended to reflect the problems and difficulties of their own prisons rather than grievance procedures in general. For example, a governor at one of the local prisons had experienced difficulties in the way in which some of its inmates' medical problems had been dealt with in the past and felt that access to outside doctors should be made easier. One of the governors at a dispersal prison raised questions about the wings having telephones and about the censoring of mail. Governors at one of the training prisons felt that its short sentence inmates weren't always aware of the channels of complaint open to them, while another felt that long term inmates should be given training in problem mediation as in the United States.

Thus governors' criticisms tended to be miscellaneous and directed at aspects of central Home Office policy rather than clustered around problems of local grievance procedures. A possible exception was the suggestion made by a

31

governor at one of the local prisons that grievance procedures at his prison should be less formal, in particular that governors be more accessible to inmates. One of his colleagues suggested that there should be a 'surgery' manned by members of the Board of Visitors, the Local Review Committee, staff and governors, which could discuss matters of inmate concern informally. He felt that this was particularly important in local prisons because inmates had to be locked up for so much of the day. However, as the first governor pointed out, the factors that made such an innovation desirable also made it difficult to achieve—"in locals all movement has to be co-ordinated so that easy access to governors would interfere with the running of establishments and staff would feel threatened". Nevertheless, the fact that the problem was articulated was interesting, particularly when considered in the context of the critical comments made by inmates about grievance procedures in local prisons (see page 36).

Boards of Visitors

While governors were not very critical of their own role in grievance procedures, they were reasonably clear about what they considered to be the shortcomings of the Board of Visitors and the petition system. Their main criticism of the Board of Visitors was that it needed to have a more critical attitude when dealing with inmates' grievances. As one Governor said, "I constantly urge them not to worry about me and to be more critical and get on with their job". Another recounted how an inmate had complained that he had not had a full visit and how Board members had accepted too readily the Governor's reason that it was due to insufficient staff. Altogether, almost half the sample of governors interviewed mentioned this need for a more critical attitude.

The petition system

With respect to petitions, the majority of governors felt that the Home Office's replies were inadequate in terms of their speed (52%) and, more particularly, in terms of their detail (74%). When governors were asked how they felt petition replies could be improved, their main suggestions were that the style of reply should be more personal (34%) and that more reasons should be given as to why the decision had been reached (25%).

The nature and level of petitioning

Governors were also asked why, in their opinion, some of the requests and grievances referred to them became petitions and if the level of petitions from their prison could be significantly reduced. They confirmed that most of the requests and grievances which became petitions did so either because they concerned matters which only the Home Office was empowered to deal with (compulsory referrals), or they concerned matters that were traditionally referred to the Home Office for central decision (customary referrals). Otherwise, petitions were usually the result of an inmate being unwilling to accept a local decision, in which case the petition acted as an appeal mechanism. Occasionally, other factors were mentioned such as using the petition as a way of avoiding an impasse or dealing with a particularly obstinate complainant.

Because of the 'compulsory referral', 'customary referral' or 'appeal' nature of petitions, most governors felt that the level of petitioning could not be significantly reduced—although some marginal effect might be achieved by modifying particular management procedures. For example, an assistant governor at one of the local prisons suggested that if all requests to petition were channelled through the Governor then the level might be reduced as the Governor was often able to discuss inmates' problems with them and persuade them not to petition. Some governors at the training and dispersal prisons also pointed out that the level might be marginally reduced if they strictly adhered to the '28 day rule' concerning the submission of additional petitions.

However, some governors queried whether the level of petitions should be reduced—even if these sorts of procedural changes made it theoretically possible. They argued that prisoners have a right to petition and that a good system should allow them to exercise this right freely rather than discourage it or make it more difficult. The Governor of one of the prisons also made an interesting management point when he said: "they (petitions) are also important for Governors. I want HQ to tell me whether I'm right or wrong, it makes people see I am not the last recourse and that my decisions are open to inspection; the work of Governors is not overviewed sufficiently in my opinion".

Apart from the slight reduction which these procedural changes might produce, governors were agreed that any decrease in the level of petitioning could only be achieved by allowing some of the subjects that presently required 'customary' referral to be dealt with locally: most frequently mentioned was permission to have photographs taken and sent out (one prison had asked the Home Office that this should become a matter for Governor's discretion), and several governors also argued that compensation for lost or damaged property (where the prison accepts responsibility) should also be a matter for local management. A variety of other subjects were also suggested including productions at court, unopposed inter-regional transfer requests, back pay, extra visits to dying relatives, etc. However, it was accepted that such selective delegation would make little difference to the overall level of petitioning; the proportion of such petitions was small, and the proportion supported by local management was even smaller.

Some governors argued that there was a case for limiting the petition to its appeal function, and managing its request functions some other way; for example, transfer requests could be dealt with by memoranda, parole problems could be addressed directly to the Parole Unit at the Prison Department, problems about sentence and conviction could be dealt with directly by

Criminal Department, etc. It was acknowledged that such separation would make no difference to the total number of requests and grievances submitted to the Home Office and that the same subjects would still be dealt with by the same sections. The purpose of the separation would be to relate the procedure more directly to inmates' grievances about treatment and conditions in prison rather than their objections to the criminal justice system as a whole.

Boards of Visitors' views on grievance procedures

The majority of the 24 Board of Visitors members interviewed felt they were not familiar enough with either local grievance procedures or the petition system to offer views on these and confined their views to their own role in grievance procedures. They felt their unique contribution was that of being a 'sympathetic listener' and an 'independent watchdog' rather than in the resolution of grievances. They described themselves as making "the inmate feel his case is considered sympathetically, albeit we can't always be effective" and spoke in terms of "our independence of the prison management, our freedom of entry and exit and our publicity potential".

Board members were divided about whether or not inmates made sufficient use of them in ventilating their requests and grievances. As Table 9 shows, Board members at dispersals felt themselves to be more fully used by inmates than did Board members at the other prisons. For example, a member at one of the local prisons stated: "I notice when I take applications that queues start to form, indicating a potential market". On the other hand, a member at one of the dispersal prisons commented: "judging from the numbers I see, I should say I am fully used, although they don't consider us independent of the establishment".

Table 9

Board Members' views on whether they felt themselves to be adequately used by inmates, by type of prison

Members' views	Local	Training	Dispersal
Adequately used	1	2	5
Under used	4	4	1
Undecided	3	4	2

There were similar inter-prison differences when members were asked whether, in their opinion, inmates considered them to be sufficiently independent, members at dispersal prisons being noticeably more confident in this respect (Table 10).

Table 10
Board Members' views on whether inmates considered them to be independent

Members' views	Local	Training	Dispersal
Inmates consider us independent	—	—	4
Inmates do not consider us independent	6	3	3
Undecided	2	3	1
Missing data	—	2	—

The same pattern emerged with respect to the general confidence of Board members in the ability of inmates to recognise them and understand their role in grievance procedures: this was greater at dispersal prisons than the other prisons (Table 11).

Table 11
Board Members' views about inmate ability to recognise them and understand their role in grievance procedures

Members' views	Local	Training	Dispersal
Inmates recognise us and understand our role	2	1	4
Inmates don't recognise us or are unclear about our role	5	3	1
Undecided	1	—	3
Missing data	—	4	—

Members' own views about their independence revealed a certain amount of ambiguity. While a clear majority (67%) said they felt reasonably independent of the Governor in dealing with applications, a majority also felt that they had to support him in general—partly because of his responsibility for the discipline and security of the prison, and partly because of the need to maintain confidence in each other.

Board members' suggestions for improving their role reflected some of these concerns. For example, just under a quarter of their suggestions concerned ways of improving inmates' perceptions of their independence, the most common suggestion being that governors and uniformed staff should not be present when applications were being taken; these suggestions for improving independence were most typical of members at local prisons.*

Suggestions for improving the Boards' 'visibility' were also most common amongst members at the local prisons, as were suggestions that panels or clinics should replace single members and Board meetings for taking applications. Members at the dispersal prisons seemed to be more concerned with

---

* In fact, it is open to any Board member to receive an application out of sight and hearing of staff.

widening the background and qualifications of Board members and increasing the amount of time that could be devoted to dealing with prisoners' grievances. Table 12 summarises the 45 different suggestions made by the members interviewed.

Table 12
Board members' suggestions for improving their role

Suggestion	Local	Training	Dispersal
Improved perception of independence (eg staff should not be present when applications are being taken)	8	3	—
Wider Board membership	4	—	4
More panels or clinics	5	3	—
Improved effectiveness (eg improved feedback to inmates)	2	4	1
Improved visibility of Boards	6	—	—
More time to deal with applications	—	1	4

Inmates' views on grievance procedures

i. Inmates' confidence in procedures at wing and governor levels

The sample of 202 inmates who had recently submitted or withdrawn petitions were asked two questions which tried to establish the level of confidence they had in the way in which staff dealt with their requests and grievances. The first question asked them who they had seen about their problem and whether they had found them helpful or not. The responses to the latter part of this question were often confused: inmates would often identify helpfulness with the success or otherwise of their application rather than with factors such as the amount and quality of the advice they received, the extent and promptness of any action, the attitude of the member of staff etc. Moreover, what one inmate might consider to be a helpful response might not be so considered by another. Nevertheless, the pattern of responses varied considerably between types of prison. The second question was a more general open-ended question which asked inmates what they thought of the way in which requests and complaints were dealt with generally at their prison. This produced a great deal of material, much of it of limited relevance and often subjective. However, the pattern of responses also varied noticeably from one type of prison to another; it also included a considerable number of approbatory statements.

Local prisons

Confidence in grievance procedures at wing and governor levels was lowest at the two local prisons with little apparent difference between them in this respect. The characteristic problems of local prisons—rapid turnover of population, commitment of staff to court duties, long lock-up periods, etc—meant that staff were unable to devote sufficient time and resources to dealing with inmates' requests and complaints in any depth. Inevitably, these limitations were reflected in inmates' responses. Only a small proportion of the sample felt that their requests and grievances had been dealt with at all positively or sympathetically by wing staff or governor grades. Mostly they felt that their applications had been dealt with matter-of-factly or off-handedly and that staff were uninterested and sometimes hostile.

Their comments about the way in which complaints were dealt with generally at the prison were even more critical. Only eight out of the total sample of 56 inmates at the two prisons expressed appreciative (or at least neutral) views about the way staff dealt with problems. The overwhelming majority of the inmates interviewed expressed dissatisfaction with their treatment. Among the more severe statements were threats to take legal action about supposed lack of medical treatment and assertions such as "staff don't treat you as prisoners, but as dogs—you have to keep pestering if you want anything". Even allowing for the inevitable elements of hostility and resentment inherent in staff/prisoner relationships, the degree of dissatisfaction expressed by inmates at the two local prisons with grievance procedures at staff levels was very striking.

Training prisons

Confidence in grievance procedures at staff level was much higher at the training prisons. It was noticeably high at Training 1, a significant finding in view of the prison's demanding and volatile population. Few of its sample of 40 inmates reported being dissatisfied with the quality of help they had received with their individual problems at wing or duty governor level. This confidence was not simply a reflection of the fact that a large proportion of petitions concerned parole and sentence and conviction—subjects which staff feel free to offer advice and sympathy about—as strong confidence was also apparent in their views of how grievances were dealt with generally at the prison: "this prison is terrific for dealing with people's problems", "there's no problem—they advise you, they're quite helpful here" were two of the more glowing testimonials in this respect.

Confidence in general grievance procedures at staff levels were also high at Training 2, although there was more criticism about how their individual problems had been dealt with, particularly at duty governor level. However, most criticisms was reserved for what they claimed to be the inaccessibility of the Governor: "getting to see the No 1 in this prison is like going to the other side of the moon", "wing staff won't let you see him; you have to beg to see the assistant governor, let alone the No 1" were some of the comments made about this. None of the 26 inmates interviewed at Training 2 had seen the Governor in connection with their problem, compared with 11 out of 40 at Training 1. However, these criticisms did not imply a belief that easier access to the Governor would necessarily result in a more favourable decision being made.

Dispersal prisons

Confidence in grievance procedures at staff level also seemed to be high at the two dispersals, both in respect of the help which inmates received with their particular problems and the way staff dealt with complaints generally. A criticism at Dispersal 2 concerned the perceived inaccessibility of the Governor. As at Training 2 the desire to see the Governor arose from a point of perceived 'principle' rather than a belief that it would make much difference to the outcome of the application.

ii. Inmates' confidence in Boards of Visitors

The sample of 202 inmates who had recently submitted or withdrawn petitions were asked whether they had previously seen the Board of Visitors about their request or complaint, and if not, why not. The question produced a large number of observations about the Board and its role in grievance procedures, some of limited relevance and some difficult to interpret. A limitation of the exercise concerned the nature of the sample: many of the subjects raised by the sample would not normally have been referred to the Board anyway, for example those concerning parole, deportation, sentence and conviction and requests for compensation. In such cases the Board has very little power or influence and this was often the reason given by inmates for not making use of it. Nevertheless, the inmates concerned often gave other or additional reasons for not consulting them which made it possible to identify and analyse their basic criticisms of the Board.

Local prisons

Only five of the 26 inmates interviewed at the two local prisons had made any use of the Board in connection with their requests or grievances. Their comments were fairly critical: one prisoner complained 'the member was about to reply when the accompanying officer interrupted and said that the issue was for the governor'. Another inmate claimed that he had withdrawn his petition (concerning a Governor's adjudication award) in order to see the Board and was then advised by them to petition.

Being local prisons, the petitions were mostly concerned with problems of transfer and allocation, subjects rarely suitable for Board intervention. However, few inmates claimed that this was the reason for not consulting them. Mostly their reasons reflected either a lack of faith in the Board's independence or a more general ignorance about the Board's role and function in grievance procedures. The Board's supposed lack of independence was mentioned by about one quarter of the sample, the most common criticism being that its decisions were unduly influenced by the Governor and prison staff.

The Board's adjudicatory role was also mentioned as a reason for doubting its independence, but it seemed to be much less important to the inmates than the Board's identification with the Governor and prison authority generally.

Given the rapid turnover of population and the large proportion of first sentence offenders at the two local prisons, a significant degree of ignorance about the Board's role and procedures was not unexpected. It was noticeably high at Local 2 however, where comments such as "I didn't know whether I was entitled (to see them)" and "I didn't know what he (the officer) meant by visiting magistrates" were very common.

Training prisons

The sample of inmates interviewed at the two training prisons had a more sophisticated knowledge of the Board and its role. For example, many of them knew that there was little or nothing the Board could do about matters concerning parole, deportation, conviction and sentence, compensation, security classification etc; 19 out of the sample of 66 men interviewed gave this as the reason for not applying to the Board. But, as at the local prisons, there were a large number of complaints about the Board's supposed lack of independence, both in respect of the Governor and in respect of its adjudicatory role. As at the local prisons, however, it was the Board's perceived identification with the Governor and prison staff generally that seemed to concern the men most. Fifteen of the 19 men mentioned this aspect compared with only four who emphasised its disciplinary function. A proportion of the sample complained that the Board was not powerful enough, not so much in the sense of being unable to deal with particular subject matters, but in the sense of being generally ineffective and uninterested. A number of miscellaneous reasons were also given for not seeing the Board, such as the matter being too trivial, the wish to avoid complaining, and a belief that the Board was out of touch with the realities of prison life.

Dispersal prisons

The sample of inmates at Dispersal 2 had made more use of the Board than the sample at Dispersal 1, nine out of 40 consulting them compared with three out of 40. The reasons for the difference are not clear, particularly as few of the 12 inmates concerned claimed to have found their intervention helpful. However, it may be of note that far fewer inmates at Dispersal 2 criticised the Board for its supposed lack of independence than was the case at Dispersal 1. Amongst those who did make this criticism it was, once again, the Board's identification with the Governor and prison authority generally that concerned them rather than its disciplinary role.

Being dispersal prisoners, few of the men were ignorant about the role of the Board and most of their other reasons for not consulting the Board concerned its lack of powers, either in the sense of their request or complaint being outside its jurisdiction or in the sense of it lacking sufficient weight and authority to affect decisions made by prison staff.

iii. Inmates' experience and views of the petition system

Inmates' confidence in the petition system as a procedure for dealing with their requests and complaints was one of the main concerns of the study. Accordingly, as previously noted, the sample of inmates had been structured to represent the views of different groups of inmates who had recently had different experiences of the procedure. One group, the 'petitioners', had submitted petitions and had received replies to them. Another group, the 'withdrawns', had decided to petition but in the event had not persisted with this intention: they may have either been satisfied with the action taken on their complaint, or they may have been persuaded by staff to withdraw it, or they may have simply lost interest. Sometimes the petition was written out and processed locally before it was withdrawn, and sometimes it was simply left uncompleted or was 'lost' by the inmate. To some extent the distinction between the two groups was artificial; many 'petitioners' had withdrawn petitions in the past and similarly many 'withdrawns' had recently been 'petitioners'. Nevertheless, it was considered worth retaining the distinction to see if any differences in attitude emerged. The final group, the 'non-petitioners', were inmates who had not petitioned from their current prison for at least six months. This group was included in order to investigate the possibility that those inmates who had made use of the petition procedure might not be representative of the general run of inmates.

It had been intended to interview 50 inmates at each of the six prisons in the sample—20 petitioners, 20 withdrawns and 10 non-petitioners. In the event, it was not always possible to achieve full samples of the last two groups. Because of their different experiences of the petition system, the views of the three groups are dealt with separately.

(a) Inmates who had recently petitioned

The sample of 120 petitioners were asked why they had decided to petition, what sort of reply they had expected to receive from the Home Office and what they thought of the reply they had actually received. They were also asked whether they would petition again, either about the same subject or about something different.

Reasons for petitioning

The majority of petitions had been submitted because the subject matter required the inmate to make a formal request. Although most of these formal request-type petitions were of the 'compulsory referral' sort, about one sixth were of the 'customary referral' sort (see p. 3). Transfer requests occupied a somewhat ambiguous position in this respect. The number of establishments to which the allocation unit of a local prison can send an inmate (ie taking into account security category and length of sentence) is usually very limited. Consequently, decisions about allocations are not local decisions in the same way as are decisions about privileges and local conditions, and appeals against such decisions cannot really be classified as appeals against local decisions either. Table 13 gives the type and subject matter of the petitions forwarded by the six prisons. It shows that appeals against allocation decisions and requests for transfer were by far the most common subjects at the local prisons, while problems concerning parole and sentence and conviction accounted for the majority of petitions forwarded from the training prisons. The dispersal prisons showed more variation, although the geographical position of Dispersal 1 was responsible for a large number of requests for transfer from this prison.

Table 13
Type of petition forwarded by subject and by prison

Type and subject	Local 1	2	Training 1	2	Dispersal 1	2	Total
COMPULSORY REFERRAL							
Parole	1	—	9	11	3	4	28
Sentence and conviction	—	—	5	—	—	1	6
Other	1	—	1	—	—	—	2
Sub-total	2	—	15	11	3	5	36
CUSTOMARY REFERRAL							
Compensation for lost/damaged property	—	1	—	1	—	2	4
Requests for photos	—	—	—	—	1	2	3
Home leave/temporary release	—	—	1	1	3	—	5
Production at court	2	—	2	—	—	—	4
Other	—	1	—	—	4	—	5
Sub-total	2	2	3	2	8	4	21
APPEALS AGAINST LOCAL DECISIONS							
Diet	—	—	—	—	—	1	1
Medical treatment	1	—	—	1	—	1	3
Disciplinary awards	1	1	—	—	—	2	4
Other	1	—	—	1	2	2	6
Sub-total	3	1	1	3	—	6	14
ALLOCATION AND TRANSFER PROBLEMS	12	17	1	4	8	5	47
MISCELLANEOUS	1	—	—	—	1	—	2
TOTAL	20	20	20	20	20	20	120

The petition files of the inmates in the sample were subsequently examined in order to assess the extent to which staff had supported their petitions. Making

41

use of this material and the reasons given by inmates for submitting petitions, it was possible to conclude that few, if any, petitions resulted from arbitrary or poorly considered local decisions. Moreover, while it might be argued that a considerable number of petitions were 'time wasting' in the sense of having little or no chance of success (for example the large number of unsupported transfer requests) this was not how they were regarded by the inmates: a large number really did believe that they might be successful and others considered that they should try every means of protest available to them.

The number of requests and grievances which were supported by staff, but which they were not empowered to grant, were very few: there was a request for compensation for a damaged radio (the prison having accepted liability and being prepared to pay), a request by an inmate to have a photograph taken and sent to his family, two requests to attend civil proceedings at court, a request to visit a sick wife and two requests for transfer (one of which was arranged by the prison after the petition had been submitted), some seven petitions in all.

Thus, the potential for reducing the overall number of petitions submitted to the Home Office, either by improved procedures or by increased delegation, would seem to be very little. As previously noted, Prison Department had argued this very point to the Home Affairs Committee in 1980 and the evidence of the present sample seems to justify their position.

Petitioners' expectations of replies

Additional support for this point of view can be drawn from the sample's expectations about the outcome of their petitions. More than half the sample (71 out of 120) claimed that they had expected a favourable reply to their petition. As most inmates are aware that few petitions are granted, (and a large number of the sample expressed very cynical views about the petitioning system in general), this degree of optimism was rather striking.

The populations of the training and dispersal prisons might have been expected to have been more cynical about the possible outcome of their petitions, but the type of prison seemed to make no difference. This finding may be partly due to the fact that very often the favourable expectation appeared to arise from a conviction that the request was reasonable and justified, rather than an actual consideration of the realities involved: "I wasn't asking for much, there are always spare seats on the vans when they go to London" (transfer for visits) and "I had hoped for 18 months back because I had got a good case" (restoration of lost remission) were characteristic remarks.

Those who did not expect a favourable reply but still persisted with their petition did so for a variety of reasons. A large proportion simply felt that it was worth a try; a number felt it was partly a matter of principle as well, and others indicated that they saw the petition as a procedural device which gave them access to other external avenues of redress (chiefly by allowing them to write to MPs). There were also a number of miscellaneous reasons such as "I told my wife I'd had a 'knock back' (parole refusal)—99 out of a hundred men feel bitter about that: my wife said 'is that it' and I said I could petition— she said 'do it'".

Petitioners' satisfaction with the types of replies received

Only six petitioners received a favourable reply from the Home Office to their request or grievance: one petition was a straightforward request to attend a magistrates' court hearing for guardianship proceedings; another was a request for an early parole review on the grounds that the inmate's co-defendant (who had received an identical sentence) had been granted parole. The third inmate requested a transfer to a prison nearer his home on the grounds that it would facilitate visits from his family. The fourth petitioner requested a transfer for accumulated visits and to have photographs of himself sent out to relations who could not visit him since they lived in Australia and Scotland. The fifth case was more routine: it concerned an application for back pay whilst on remand at Brixton. The final case was a request for compensation for a radio which had been damaged during a cell search. All but one of these petitions had been accompanied by a supportive report from prison staff: in the remand case, the prison, while not supporting the application, had raised no objections.

The speed with which the sample of petitions had been considered did not seem to be a problem. Equal numbers of petitioners were satisfied, dissatisfied, or had had no particular views on the issue (30%, 30% and 28% respectively). Interestingly, 11% felt that their petition had been dealt with too quickly and half of these expressed doubts as to whether their petition had left the prison at all. For example, an inmate who had requested a review of his security categorisation and who had received a quick reply commented that the processing seemed "unusually quick—I felt they hadn't considered it". Another inmate who had requested a transfer and who had received a reply within days complained "It only took 10 days I did not think it had left the jail".

Inmates' reactions to the contents of petition replies were much more critical. A significant proportion of petitioners felt that the replies they had received were too impersonal and stereotyped or had not been properly considered. However, their predominant criticism was that the Home Office gave no reasons for their decisions, and when they were asked about the detail contained in petition replies, the overwhelming majority felt it to be insufficient. In the words of one respondent, "the Home Office are defensive to hide behind a photo-copied answer; no doubt they have reasons on file—even the Appeal Court gives reasons for refusals".

Future petitioning intentions

In order to establish whether they had been influenced by their experiences of petitioning, the sample was asked whether they would petition again (either about the same subject or about something else). Predicting future behaviour is of course somewhat hazardous: the sample of inmates was aware that circumstances could alter and affect their present attitudes. Nevertheless, the majority of the sample (57%) said that they might well petition again. In view of the sample's general cynicism about the effectiveness of petitioning, the high proportion of inmates prepared to continue using the system was unexpected; it was, however, consistent with the 'customary' and 'compulsory' referral nature of many petitions, and the high proportion of petitioners who had expected a favourable reply to their request. Thus, both popular opinion and individual experience of petitioning appeared to have little or no effect on actual petitioning 'behaviour', at least in respect of intentions and expectations.

The sample were asked for the reasons why they would or would not petition again. A principal consideration, mentioned by 16 (13%) of the inmates, was the Home Office's rejection of their petition: they either had re-petitioned or were considering re-petitioning about the same subject. In some cases, this intention reflected their commitment to their cause, while in other cases it reflected a belief that they were now in a position to put forward a better case. There was also the intention to petition again as a procedural device: "I shall petition about the same subject so I can write to my MP and Lord Elton" or because of dissatisfaction with the Home Office's response to the initial petition.

In the remaining cases, inmates' reasons for considering petitioning again were not so directly related to the rejection of their petition; rather, they seemed to reflect the particular characteristics of the petitioner and petition system in general. For some inmates, petitioning was clearly a matter of principle: "it's my duty to tell the Home Office about injustice, it's the principle behind it", was one striking example of this attitude. In general, however, the notion of principle was expressed more provisionally, the inmate claiming he would petition again if "it was serious enough" or "if there was a good reason".

As against this 'principled' approach, a considerable number of inmates spoke of petitioning as a procedure which they would only use in certain circumstances, especially following a refusal to grant parole. Other circumstances occasionally mentioned concerned money matters, time wasting possibilities and a desire to exhaust all possible avenues.

The majority of those who said they would not petition again indicated a general lack of faith in the system. Their most common verdict was that the procedure was a waste of time, primarily because of the refusals they had experienced themselves or seen other inmates experience. Others emphasised their belief that the system was not independent. A large number of these inmates accompanied their statement of a general lack of faith in the system with declarations that they would use other means of protest next time. The options mentioned ranged from legal action against staff and using the media, to more individual types of protest such as hunger strikes and violence. One or two inmates said they wouldn't petition again because they wanted to avoid trouble. Table 14 summarises the reasons which inmates gave for why they might, or might not, petition again. However, because some inmates gave several reasons, while others gave rather obscure reasons, the categories and numbers should both be regarded as indicative rather than precise.

Table 14
Petitioners' reasons for why they might, or might not petition again

Intention and reason	Local	Training	Dispersal	Total
WOULD PROBABLY PETITION AGAIN				
Dissatisfaction with petition reply	6	4	6	16
As a point of 'principle'	4	6	6	16
If certain circumstances arise (specified and unspecified)	1	6	10	17
To make work for staff	3	1	1	5
Psychological	3	—	1	4
As a procedural device	1	1	2	4
Miscellaneous	2	3	1	6
Sub-Total	20	21	27	68
WOULD PROBABLY NOT PETITION AGAIN				
No faith in the system	11	10	7	28
Do not want any trouble	2	1	1	4
General acquiescence	1	1	1	3
Miscellaneous	2	6	3	11
Sub-Total	16	18	12	46
TOTAL	36	39	39	114

(b)   Inmates who had recently withdrawn petitions

Table 15 gives the type and subject matter of the 82 petitions which were withdrawn by inmates at their own request. Most of their petitions were concerned with transfers and parole. However, these accounted for a smaller proportion of the total sample than was the case with the petitioners; 29% as compared with 63%. The sample was also characterised by a predominance of subject matters in which governors could intervene effectively; for example, visits, pay and employment, diet and 'local treatment'.

45

Table 15
Type of petition withdrawn by subject and by prison

Type and subject	Local		Training		Dispersal		Total
	1	2	1	2	1	2	
COMPULSORY REFERRAL							
Parole	—	—	5	3	1	—	9
Sentence and conviction	—	—	1	—	—	1	2
Sub-total	—	—	6	3	1	1	11
CUSTOMARY REFERRAL							
Compensation for lost/damaged property	—	—	1	—	1	1	3
Back pay	—	—	1	—	1	2	4
Requests for photos	—	—	—	—	—	1	1
Home leave/temporary release	—	—	—	—	—	1	1
Others	—	—	—	—	1	—	1
Sub-total	—	—	2	—	4	4	10
APPEALS AGAINST LOCAL DECISIONS							
Diet	1	—	2	—	—	4	7
Medical treatment	3	—	1	1	1	3	9
Disciplinary awards	—	1	2	—	—	2	5
Visits	—	1	2	—	2	—	5
Local treatment and conditions	—	3	1	—	2	2	8
Other	—	—	3	—	4	2	9
Sub-total	4	5	11	1	9	13	43
ALLOCATION AND TRANSFER PROBLEMS	2	5	—	2	6	—	15
MISCELLANEOUS	—	—	1	—	—	2	3
TOTAL	6	10	20	6	20	20	82

Reasons for withdrawing petitions

The inmates in the sample were asked why they had withdrawn their petitions. A number were withdrawn simply because the inmate's circumstances had changed or altered in a way which made the petition redundant or unnecessary: one inmate had been given his parole date (which made a transfer request unnecessary); another had become eligible for parole after staff had checked the matter, and another inmate withdrew his petition for transfer when his wife divorced him, and the need for the move had been removed.

However, of the petitions withdrawn at the inmate's instigation, the most frequently given reason was satisfaction with some form of action or intervention by prison staff; this was given as the main reason by some 27% of the sample of 82 withdrawns and as a subsidiary reason by several others. For example, an inmate had complained that a visit from his girlfriend had been cut short and that he had decided to petition about it: "I was called up to the Chief's office about two hours after handing it (petition) in and he explained the rules and procedures of petitioning. He said he was willing to give me another visiting order and was I willing to withdraw my petition". In another case, an inmate claimed that his mail was being improperly censored and that he was going to petition about it. However, his complaint was investigated and "I was given an undertaking by the principal officer that he would carpet the censor and that my mail would not be interfered with". Several cases concerned medical problems—inmates claiming that they had received inadequate or incorrect medical attention and then being sufficiently assured or satisfied by subsequent action to withdraw their petitions. For example, one inmate complained that his treatment was not in accordance with his outside specialist's instructions; once he had obtained a petition form he was granted access to the senior medical officer, and it was agreed that he should receive the specified treatment. Another inmate withdrew his petition when he had been issued with a pair of special surgical boots that he had been asking for. In many of these cases inmates clearly believed, probably with some justification, that their petitions had been instrumental, or at least helpful, in getting their complaint or grievance redressed.

While not being satisfied with action taken, some inmates admitted being satisfied with the explanations or persuasions of staff. However, a comparable number of inmates indicated that they had withdrawn their petitions because they felt that the procedure was unlikely to help them very much, a lack of faith which reflected either their own experiences or those of other inmates. One inmate put it forcefully when he said "I was fighting a losing battle... the Home Office has given governors the power to run prisons more or less as they want, so petitioning would have been a waste of time". A number claimed that they had lost interest, either in the sense that they had asked for the petition in a moment of temper and then cooled down, or in the sense that they simply couldn't be bothered to pursue the matter any further.

A number of inmates also claimed that they withdrew their petitions because they did not want to create trouble. In some cases this was because of the kind of action which they thought might be taken against them: "they said 'name the officers or withdraw', but naming officers makes you liable to legal proceedings and there was no way I was doing that—so I withdrew". Another inmate said "the officers told me I'd be in serious trouble if I kept on with my hunger strike and making trouble and not conforming etc and that I would be sent to Stafford—and there's no way I want to go to Stafford".

There were also the miscellaneous cases, such as the inmate who had been advised by his solicitors not to petition but to take legal remedies instead, or

47

the example already mentioned (see page 38) of the inmate who had withdrawn his petition in order to see the Board of Visitors, and was then told to petition.

Table 16 summarises the sample's reasons for withdrawing their petitions. As with the other tables of this kind it should be borne in mind that inmates often gave several reasons for their decisions and that the various categories and numbers should therefore be treated as broad indications, rather than accurate enumerations, of their feelings.

Table 16
Withdrawns reasons for withdrawing their petitions

Reason	Local	Training	Dispersal	Total
Satisfaction with action taken by staff	8	6	8	22
No faith in the system	—	6	13	19
Loss of interest	—	5	6	11
Wish to avoid trouble	3	3	4	10
Persuasion by staff	3	—	3	6
Change in circumstances	—	3	3	6
Miscellaneous	2	3	3	8
Total	16	26	40	82

The sample of withdrawns at the two local prisons was very small so that inter-prison comparisons are difficult to make. However, the proportion of petitions withdrawn because of satisfaction with action taken seems to have been comparatively large at the locals. Analysis showed that this was because inmates at these prisons often had limited knowledge of petitioning procedures (and prison routine in general) and frequently put them in unnecessarily. It was therefore often possible for staff either to take action or persuade them to withdraw.

Future petitioning intentions

Like the petitioners, the withdrawns were asked whether they might petition in the future. Some 80% out of the sample of 82 indicated that they might, ranging from those who only rated it as a vague possibility to those who had actually petitioned again. This proportion was even larger than that of the petitioners, confirming that inmates' readiness to use the procedure bore little relation to the general cynicism with which it was regarded. The main reason for this discrepancy was that future petitioning depended on circumstances: many matters could only be dealt with by means of a petition (the 'customary' and 'compulsory' referral nature of the system). Thus, readiness to use the procedure tended to reflect inmates' assessment of how likely these problems were to arise in future, rather than their faith in the system's ability to redress their grievances. The next largest group of reasons for withdrawing petitions clustered around the idea of the principle involved.

The remaining 20% of the sample of withdrawns indicated they would probably not use the petition procedure again (see Table 17). Like the petitioners, most of the reasons they gave indicated a general lack of faith in the system, for example that it was a waste of time, that the Home Office was not independent or concerned enough, that they had had too many refusals in the past. Very often these opinions were coupled with an apparent determination to use other means of protest in future, such as a Parliamentary petition or letters to the media. As before, a number of inmates said they wouldn't petition because they thought it might rebound on them in some way, and some just wanted a quiet life.

Table 17
Withdrawns reasons for why they might, or might not, petition again

Intention and reason	Local	Training	Dispersal	Total
MIGHT PETITION AGAIN				
If certain circumstances arise (specified and unspecified)	5	6	18	29
Because of the principle involved	5	3	6	14
As a procedural device	3	2	4	9
For psychological reasons	—	1	2	3
To create work for staff	1	1	—	2
Previous positive experiences	—	2	1	3
Miscellaneous	—	3	3	6
Sub-total	14	18	34	66
WOULD PROBABLY NOT PETITION AGAIN				
No faith in the system	—	6	4	10
Do not want any trouble	1	—	2	3
General acquiescence	1	2	—	3
Sub-total	2	8	6	16
TOTAL	16	26	40	82

(c)   Inmates with little or no recent experience of petitioning

Fifty-five inmates who had not recently petitioned were interviewed as a control group for the sample of 'petitioners' and 'withdrawns'. In order to establish their comparability with the other two samples, they were asked whether or not anything had recently happened at the prison which had annoyed them. The large majority had felt annoyed at something and most of these had made an application about the matter. Thus, it was possible to conclude that non-petitioners were not notably acquiescent. This was further supported by the answers to another question. When asked "although you

49

haven't petitioned, have you recently taken a request, complaint, or problem to a governor here?'', 33% reported that they had.

Consequently, the non-petitioning behaviour of the sample could not be attributed either to having fewer things to complain about or to having a greater degree of tolerance than the other two groups. Accordingly, they were asked whether there had been any particular reason why they had not put in a petition in the preceding six months. Respondents gave three principal reasons. A considerable number (33%) had not petitioned because they had had no particular reason to. A similar number said that the petition system was a 'waste of time', largely because of the expectation of negative replies. Many (24%) expressed a general apprehension about the possible result of such action; they felt that it might delay their release date, damage their parole chances or result in them being labelled as 'trouble-makers'.

Inmates' use of alternatives to petitioning

During initial fieldwork at the training prisons, it was found that a proportion of the inmates interviewed had previously used, or were currently using, other means of airing their grievances, generally by writing to their MPs, but also by writing to other bodies such as the Howard League, the NCCL and Justice. As a result, it was decided to introduce a question about the use of such alternatives in the inmate interviews at the remaining four prisons. This meant that comparisons could only be made between the two local and two dispersal prisons, but because the samples included both petitioners and withdrawns (and were therefore fairly large), it was felt to be a worthwhile exercise. Table 18 gives the numbers of petitioners and withdrawns who reported using alternative avenues of airing their grievances, in connection with current or past grievances.

Table 18
Petitioners and withdrawns use of alternative avenues to petitioning

When used	Local		Dispersal		Total
	1	*2*	*1*	*2*	
With current or past grievances	1	7	3	9	20
With past grievance only	5	2	9	14	30
No reported usage	20	21	28	17	86
Total	26	30	40	40	136

Local prisons

Fifteen of the 56 petitioners and withdrawns (27%) at the two local prisons said that they had used (or were still using) other means of airing their current

50

grievances, or that they had used them in connection with past grievances. Very often the inmate had done both. The inmate's MP was by far the most common alternative avenue of complaint, either singly or as one of several other alternatives such as solicitors, doctors or the press. In many cases, the contact appears to have been initiated by the inmate's wife, girlfriend or family. One or two of the sample seemed to see this procedure as more useful than petitioning: "petitions never get OK'ed, they (MPs) do more than petitions, you know someone is representing you and you feel safer".

In addition to the 15 inmates who had actually used one or more of the alternative procedures (in the past or present), a further seven inmates claimed that they had either thought about it (and rejected the idea for a variety of reasons), or were still considering it as a possible course of action. Some of the sample claimed that they would not use these alternatives because it might create some form of trouble for them. Four inmates claimed that they didn't really know anything about the alternative procedures, one of them claiming he might use them in future now that he knew about them.

Dispersal prisons

A much larger proportion of petitioners and withdrawns at the two dispersal prisons had used alternative means of airing their past or present grievances, some 34 out of the sample of 80 (43%) reporting such usage. This, no doubt, reflected the greater experience and sophistication of the dispersal population—and the great amount of time available to them to pursue such avenues.

The inmate's MP was again by far the most common alternative, either singly or in combination with others. Sometimes the list of others could be quite long; one inmate reported that he had written to his MP, Lord Longford, the Regional Director, the Queen and Prince Charles and another said "I handed a five page statement to my wife on a visit to give to my MP and wrote to the Home Secretary, the papers, the Governor of the prison, the Director of Prison Medical Services and the Home Office".

Inmates' appraisal of MPs as an alternative to petitioning seemed to depend very much on their experience of them. Comments from two inmates with positive experiences of them were: "I've had my solicitors approach MPs, and questions have been asked (in Parliament) on several occasions" and "my wife contacted my MP about my eye condition and I got treatment at Moorfields". Sometimes the appraisal was quite striking: "two police officers have been allotted to our case as a result of the efforts of MPs; the fact that we have got somewhere is because people outside have fought for us, not because of petitions". Others had experienced unfavourable results which also coloured their views of MPs: "I wrote to my MP and he wrote to the Home Office and just accepted their reply" and "my local MP got a letter from Mr - - saying the same thing as my reply from the Home Office".

Some inmates who had not made use of alternatives said this was because the procedure lacked independence and was generally ineffective. One inmate said "once a petition is referred that's it—an MP or anyone outside won't help, the prison system controls all complaints procedures": another expressed the same idea by saying "MPs are from the same shop as Home Office staff and I don't trust them; they never write to you with their own opinion, it's just a copy of a Home Office letter". In contrast at least six inmates who had not used alternatives indicated that they might use them in the future.

As some of the foregoing quotations indicate, the involvement of inmates' wives and girlfriends in contacting MPs, the press etc was quite striking. This was probably due to reasons of convenience on the one hand (it being easier for people outside to contact MPs and other individuals), and on the other to the fact that some inmates were referring to incidents in the past when there had been a requirement for prior investigation and petitioning before they could write to their MPs: in such cases they would often ask family or friends to contact them as a way of circumventing such requirements. But, as one inmate pointed out, it may also reflect the fact that even simultaneous ventilation requires the inmate to fully disclose the nature and details of his problem or grievance and this is not a very private process.

Home Office consideration of petitions

In order to examine the way in which the Home Office assessed the cases of the sample of petitioners, the relevant files were recalled from Prison Department and examined. Files were unobtainable for 14 of the cases and particular pieces of information were missing from some of the remaining 106 files. Consequently, the size of the sample examined varied according to the item of information being considered. The items of information analysed and the size of the relevant sample are noted below:

(i)   the time taken to reply to the petition (n = 106);

(ii) the detail of the reply (n = 96), and

(iii) the recommendations of the principal accompanying report from the prison (n = 105).

Data (i) and (ii) were used to compare staff and inmates' opinions about the speed and detail of the replies to their petitions with the actual speed and detail as recorded in the files. Data from (iii) were used to discover the proportions of petitions which were supported or not supported by the prison, and whether there was any relationship between such support and the Home Office's decision.

The average time taken to reply to the sample of petitions was 30 days. Table 19 shows that 62% of petitions received a reply within four weeks and only 13% (mostly concerned with parole) took longer than eight weeks to answer. Interestingly, the two local prisons differed from the other four prisons in that the average time of response was 20 and 36 days respectively. The quicker response for the local prisons was largely accounted for by the fact that the majority of petitions forwarded by them concerned routine and unsupported transfer requests and nearly all of these were dealt with in under four weeks.

Table 19
Time taken to reply to the petitions submitted by the sample of petitioners

Time taken to reply	Local		Training		Dispersal		Total
	1	2	1	2	1	2	
Four weeks and under	13	17	9	7	8	12	66
More than four weeks, up to and including eight weeks	2	3	7	5	7	2	26
More than eight weeks	1	—	3	5	2	3	14
Total	16	20	19	17	17	17	106

A study of inmates' satisfaction or dissatisfaction with the amount of time taken to reply to their petitions produced the unexpected finding that the number of inmates dissatisfied with 'quick' replies (ie replies which took less than four weeks) was the same as the number of inmates who said they were satisfied—23 in either case. This was because many inmates felt that a rapid response meant that their petition had not been properly considered.

With respect to the detail of petition replies, Table 20 lists the various types of reply which inmates could receive to their petitions and gives the numbers of inmates who reported they were satisfied, dissatisfied or 'neutral' with respect to each type of reply.

Table 20
Petitioners' satisfaction with replies to their petitions, by type of reply

Type	Nature	Satisfied	Neutral	Dissatisfied	Total
'expanded'	Contains some form of explanation or personalisation, subject matter mentioned	12	10	30	52
I	'fully considered', subject matter mentioned	—	2	28	30
II	'fully considered', no subject matter mentioned	1	—	5	6
III	'sympathetically considered', no subject matter mentioned	—	—	2	2
Total		13	12	65	90(*)

* Excludes six petitions that were granted (the inmates being more or less 'automatically' satisfied with the response they received).

Table 20 shows the 'expanded' reply (ie a reply which noted the subject matter of the petition and which contained some form of personalisation or explanation however brief) was the most common form of reply. A typical 'expanded' reply was:

> Your papers have been re-examined in the light of your third and fourth petition. The review of your case for parole was correctly carried out and I can assure you that it was not prejudiced in the way that you suggest. A decision was reached only after a very full and equitable assessment had been made of all the aspects of your case. The Secretary of State regrets that he is unable to justify the direction of an early review.

Approximately half the 'expanded' replies were in response to petitions about parole.

The next most commonly used form of reply was type I (33%). Like the 'expanded' reply, this reply gave the subject matter, but otherwise limited itself to a simple comment that the case had been 'fully considered', for example:

> The Secretary of State has fully considered your petition but is not prepared to grant your request for a transfer.

Most of these replies were in response to petitions requesting transfer.

The type II replies were even briefer being mostly in the format:

> The Secretary of State has fully considered your petition but can find no grounds for taking any action in regard to it.

Table 20 also shows that, overall, far more inmates were dissatisfied with the quality of the reply which they received than were satisfied, 65 (72%) and 13 (14%) respectively. This disparity was true for all types of replies; nevertheless, the proportion of inmates dissatisfied with 'expanded' replies was significantly less than the proportion dissatisfied with the remaining types of reply combined (Chi-squared = 13.3, df = 2, p<.01). This finding suggests that greater use of expanded replies would increase the proportion of inmates satisfied with the quality of reply they received from the Home Office—although only by a relatively small amount.

Nearly all the petitions were forwarded with an accompanying report prepared by a governor or principal officer. The report would usually indicate whether or not the petition was supported. When these recommendations were analysed, it was found that 14 petitions (13%) were supported and 91 (87%) were not. Only one of the 91 unsupported petitions was granted. Thus, while the petition system might be represented as a means of independent appeal against a local decision, local support would still seem necessary if the petition is to succeed. Moreover, while such support might be necessary, it is not sufficient—of the 14 petitions which were supported, the Home Office granted only six.

The analysis of petitioners' files also showed them to contain much useful material about the typical problems experienced by inmates and the responses of both local and Home Office staff. While Prison Department does monitor this information, greater use perhaps should be made of its potential for enhancing the effective management of the prison system.

Summary

Chapter 3 examined the confidence of wing staff, governors, Board members and inmates in current grievance procedures. At the two local prisons, wing application procedures were fairly formal and routine in nature. Wing staff at both prisons reported that they found the procedures to be largely satisfactory and that their routine nature made continuity of staff largely unnecessary. Procedures at the training and dispersal prisons took more time and effort and were more informal in nature. Staff at both types of prison considered applications to be an important (and sometimes satisfying) part of their job. They were also more aware of the management and control aspects of grievance procedures and frequently mentioned the importance of staff continuity at wing level.

Governors seemed fairly satisfied with their own internal procedures for dealing with inmates' requests and grievances, and the few problems they mentioned tended to reflect the particular difficulties of their own prisons rather than grievance procedures in general. They were more critical about the Board of Visitors, their main criticism being that it needed to adopt a more probing attitude towards the Governor and prison management when dealing with inmates' grievances.

Where the petition system was concerned, governors felt that petition replies were often too brief and uninformative: they felt that the style of the reply should be more personal and that more reasons should be given for the decision reached. Some governors felt that replies took too long, but this criticism was less pronounced. Most governors felt that the level of petitioning could not be significantly reduced, although a marginal effect might be achieved by modifying particular management practices or by allowing some of the subjects that presently required central referral to be dealt with locally. Additionally, some governors queried whether the level should be reduced (even if it were possible), arguing that prisoners have a right to petition and that a good system should encourage them to exercise this right freely.

Board members felt themselves to be under-used by inmates, partly because the latter were not always familiar with who Board members were and what their role was, and partly because inmates did not consider them to be sufficiently independent of prison authority when dealing with applications. Board members felt these criticisms had some justification and this was reflected in the suggestions they made for improving their role.

Inmates' confidence in staff procedures for dealing with requests and grievances was lowest at the two local prisons. Only a small proportion of the inmates interviewed felt that their problems had been dealt with at all positively or sympathetically by wing staff or governor grades. Confidence in procedures at staff levels was much higher at the training and dispersal prisons. A considerable number of inmates criticised the fact that the Governor did not normally hear governors' applications. They felt that it was important for inmates to be able to see the Governor even though they realised that it would usually make little difference to the outcome of their applications.

Very few of the inmates interviewed had made use of the Board of Visitors in connection with their request or complaint (only 17 out of the sample of 202). At the two local prisons there was a significant degree of ignorance about the Board of Visitors' role and application procedures, and one or two inmates claimed they had difficulty recognising the Board members. These comments were a reflection of the rapid turnover of population and large proportion of first sentence offenders at these prisons. At all prisons there were a large number of complaints by inmates about the Board's supposed lack of independence of the Governor and staff. This was also the most frequently given reason for not making use of the Board. The Board's adjudicatory role was also given as a reason for doubting its independence but this was much less important to inmates than the Board's general identification with the Governor and prison authority. This was true for inmates at all the six prisons in the study. Apart from the issue of independence, the most frequently given reason for not making use of the Board was its general lack of powers to deal effectively with complaints.

Inmates had little faith in the petition system; like governors, their main criticism was that the replies they received from the Home Office were inadequate and often failed to give sufficient reasons for the decisions reached. Very few received a favourable reply from the Home Office, but this seemed to have no effect on their future petitioning intentions, the majority of petitioners being prepared to petition again if necessary. The majority of withdrawns were also prepared to petition in future if necessary, their main reason being the same as that given by petitioners, that it was simply the appropriate procedure if particular problems arose or if they felt strongly about an issue. The most common reason given by inmates for withdrawing petitions at local prisons was that of satisfaction with some form of intervention or explanation by prison staff, whereas at the dispersal prisons it was lack of faith in grievance procedures.

Some 50 of the 136 inmates interviewed at the two local and two dispersal prisons said that they had used (or were still using) other means of airing their current grievance or had used them in connection with past grievances (very often they had done both). The inmate's MP was by far the most common alternative avenue of complaint, either singly or as one of several other alternatives such as solicitors, doctors or the press. The proportion of inmates using such alternatives was much greater at the dispersals than at the local prisons, reflecting the greater sophistication of the dispersal population and the greater amount of time available to them to pursue such alternatives. The role of inmates' wives and girlfriends in contacting MPs, the press, etc on behalf of inmates was also quite significant.

Non-petitioners were not noticeable for having fewer complaints or being more acquiescent than other inmates. The main reasons they gave for not petitioning were that it was a waste of time or that they had no particular reason to; a minority felt that petitioning might give them a reputation for being a trouble-maker or damage their chances of parole.

Analysis of Prison Department's processing of the sample's petitions found that the average time taken to reply to them was 30 days, reflecting the fact that a large proportion of the sample were routine and unsupported requests for transfer that were dealt with very quickly. Although governors mostly felt that the Home Office took too long to reply, inmates expressed less dissatisfaction with the speed of reply than had been expected; as many inmates were critical of 'quick' replies as were satisfied with them, the implication being that too rapid a response meant that the petition could not have been considered properly.

While staff and inmates alike felt that petition replies were often insufficiently explanatory, the analysis found that the proportion of them that were of an explanatory or expanded form was larger than this criticism suggested. Moreover, the proportion of inmates dissatisfied with this form of reply was still considerable, though much less than the proportions dissatisfied with the briefer forms of replies. This suggested that greater use of expanded replies would increase to a limited extent the proportion of inmates satisfied with the quality of answers they received from the Home Office.

Nearly all petitions were accompanied by a report prepared at principal officer or governor level, which indicated whether or not they were supported. Of the 105 petitions, some 91 were not supported and only one of these was granted. Clearly local support greatly enhances a petition's chances of succeeding, but it is not a guarantee of success. But nor is the absence of local support a guarantee of failure.

4 Implications for policy and practice

Introduction

There is no single set of criteria against which to judge the success or otherwise of the operation of a prison's grievance procedures. This is because they have to be considered within the context of the prison's regime as a whole and, in particular, as a system of activities which can complement, or interfere with, the many other aims and activities of prison management. For example, a reliable system of informing inmates about the outcome of their applications can be considered to be good practice in terms of grievance procedures, and desirable in terms of management and control because it contributes towards inmate satisfaction. Occasionally, however, the needs of the systems can diverge. For example, some members of staff argued that the use of the Governor for daily applications was both administratively inefficient and unnecessary because other members of the governor grades could do the job just as well. Although this was probably true, it was clear that many inmates set great store by having easy access to the Governor, even though they themselves were aware that it would probably make little difference to the outcome of their applications. Similarly, it can be argued that greater delegation of responsibility to basic grade officers for dealing with applications is good management practice and makes better use of existing resources. However, the inmate may not see it this way. His confidence in procedures may partly derive from the direct involvement of senior officers and governor grade staff; from his point of view greater delegation might simply make it more difficult for him to reach the levels of management he feels he ought to be dealing with and undermine his confidence in the system.

Even so, it is important to realise that grievance procedures are only one of the elements influencing inmates' general attitudes to imprisonment. For example, at both training and dispersal prisons, several inmates claimed that it was not grievance procedures as such that bothered them, but the complexities and inadequacies of the judicial system that made the process of appeal so difficult. Similarly, at the training prisons a large number of the sample were concerned with their prospects of parole to the exclusion of almost everything else. Other inmates' complaints centred round certain features of their prisons' regimes, such as having to share normal location with sex offenders, child murderers etc. Thus, no amount of excellent practices or procedures will stop some inmates from protesting their innocence or others

59

complaining about certain aspects of their prisons' regime. Nevertheless, grievance procedures are a central part of prison life and it is staff and inmate confidence in these procedures that informs the following comments.

Applications to uniformed staff and governor grades

Inmate confidence in grievance procedures at staff levels was lowest at the two local prisons. Given the limited amount of time and resources which staff can devote to grievance procedures at local prisons, this finding was not surprising, but the degree of dissatisfaction expressed was perhaps unexpected. The long lock-up periods and the rapid turnover of population made the expression of requests and grievances difficult, while at the same time the prospect of imminent allocation to a training prison (or of serving only a short sentence) may have reduced their urgency. While the functions of, and resources available to, local prisons remain under severe pressure there is probably little that can be done which would directly ameliorate this problem; however it does suggest that it is in local prisons that there is the greatest scope for improving the operation of grievance procedures. At the training and dispersal prisons, problems tend to be less pressing (in the temporal sense) and inmates also have a more elaborate network of informal staff/inmate relations which they can use when formal procedures are not operating.

A number of officers at training and dispersal prisons felt there should be more continuity of wing staff in dealing with inmates' applications but that existing arrangements for dealing with overtime equalisation had made this difficult to achieve. They emphasised the need for continuity much more than the need for special training or making greater use of basic grade officers. Staff at the local prisons argued, however, that the routine and formal nature of wing applications at local prisons made continuity unnecessary. While there may be some justification for the latter point of view, the very limited nature of staff/inmate relations at local prisons, and the low level of inmate confidence in them, would seem to make greater continuity particularly advantageous in their case, though commitment to escort and court duties would make it difficult to achieve. In general, continuity of wing staff should be an important management aim in operating and monitoring grievance procedures in prisons.

Inmates also attach considerable importance to being able to have their applications heard by the Governor. Prison Rule 8(2) states that it is the Governor who shall hear the applications of prisoners who have asked to see him. However, Rule 98 gives the Governor power to delegate any of his powers to another officer of the prison and, in practice, the responsibility for daily applications is often more or less permanently delegated to an assistant governor, on the understanding that if an inmate insists on seeing the Governor then generally he will be granted access. However, it should be borne in mind that few inmates are sufficiently assertive or confident enough to insist on such a right: this is particularly true of local prisons with their large proportion of first sentence offenders, but it is also true of prisons like Training 2 where many inmates think that such assertiveness may be mistaken for trouble-making and affect adversely their chances of parole. Inmates were also well aware that such access was unlikely to make any difference to the outcome of their applications; rather they wanted to assure themselves that they had discussed their problem with the highest authority in the prison, and could therefore regard the decision as final and definitive. From the staff's point of view, it was interesting to note that those Governors in the sample who did take daily applications were also aware of their control function, mentioning that they were a means of keeping in touch with the inmates and providing intelligence. In general, on the evidence of the six prisons, it was difficult to avoid the impression that the practice contributed positively towards inmate confidence.

Applications to Boards of Visitors

Inmates made little use of the Board of Visitors for dealing with their requests and grievances. They claimed that the Board was not independent and that it had insufficient powers. Very often they were unclear about its role in grievance procedures and some even complained that they had difficulty in recognising who its members were.

Although inmates lacked confidence in the independence of the Board, they expressed much more concern about its supposed identification with the Governor and prison authority generally, than with its adjudicatory role. Maguire and Vagg (1984) reported a similar finding and concluded that separating the watchdog and adjudicatory functions, as recommended by the Jellicoe and Justice reports, would not by itself make the Board more credible as a mechanism for dealing with grievances. While agreeing with Maguire and Vagg's point, the separation of functions and the abolition of Boards of Visitors' adjudicatory role would seem the most logical response to both sets of findings. But, irrespective of whether the Boards continue to have an adjudicatory role, it is clear that their functioning and procedures in respect of the Governor and prison authority generally need very careful consideration.

Other points which emerged from the study included the lack of privacy involved in making applications directly to members during their visits and the difficulty of knowing when members were likely to be around (and whether their part of the prison would be visited). These points were particularly evident at the two local prisons. A possible solution might be that indicated by the Jellicoe and May Committees, who strongly endorsed the system of making applications to a clinic of Board members as preferable to the system of making applications to visiting members during inspection visits. The clinic system (which is used in many training and dispersal prisons) might overcome some of these difficulties, although it does not overcome all of them.

The present study also supports Maguire and Vagg's general conclusion that Board members are seen to be insufficiently critical and interventionist in their attitude to prison authority. There was little disagreement in discussions with governors with the idea that Boards should require the Governor and staff to give a greater account of their decisions. Indeed, one Governor said he would welcome more criticism from the Board as it provided him with something to check his decisions against. As Maguire and Vagg point out, there is a widespread belief amongst Board members that they should try to 'work with' and influence the Governor rather than criticise his decisions. If, however, governors as well as inmates believe that Boards are insufficiently critical and independent of governors, then the case for examining this relationship would seem to be very strong.

The petition system

The study found that at the six prisons examined, application and petition rates tended to reflect the type of population catered for by that prison, and its general attitude towards the expression of requests and grievances, rather than particular management practices such as the delegation of responsibilities, recording practices or the existence of a 'social work in prison' policy. As a result, there appears to be little scope for reducing the overall level of petitioning. The majority of petitions were referred to the Home Office either because it alone was empowered to deal with the matter (for example problems about parole, sentence and conviction and representations against decisions to deport) or because Home Office instructions required the matter to be referred (for example requests for production at court, temporary release and permission to change one's name). Only a small proportion of the petitions forwarded were in the form of appeals against local decisions. Moreover, while governors agreed that it might be possible to reduce the appeal-type petition by changes in local practices, the reduction would only be marginal. A number of governors also emphasised that petitioning was an important right of the inmate and that they would not want to reduce it even if they could. A more substantial reduction might be achieved by giving prison staff the authority to deal with some of those matters customarily referred to the Home Office for decision. Subjects suggested by prison staff included permission to send out photographs, permission to change one's name, certain requests for production at court, certain forms of temporary release and compensation for lost or damaged property. However, analysis of the 120 petitions forwarded showed that only seven of them were both of this type and supported by staff. Thus, even if such delegation proved feasible, the reduction achieved would still be small.

The above conclusions gain support from the fact that of those petitions withdrawn by inmates, just over one half were in the form of appeals against local decisions, matters in which prison staff could effectively intervene if they felt it was justified. This was also reflected in the fact that a commonly given reason for withdrawing petitions was satisfaction with some form of action or persuasion by staff. Thus, because the submission of petitions at a local level is often effective in producing some kind of action, it is possible that it reduces both the scope and the need for central redress.

Contrary to expectations, inmate and governor dissatisfaction with the time taken to reply to petitions was not widespread. Moreover, what dissatisfaction there was amongst inmates was as much associated with rapid replies as with slow replies: inmates felt that, in the former case, the petition could not have been properly considered and might not have even left the prison. This suggests that attempts to speed up the time taken to reply to petitions, per se, will not necessarily result in greater inmate satisfaction.

The majority of both staff and inmates felt that the detail contained in petition replies was inadequate. In particular, they felt that they often gave insufficient reasons for the decisions reached. However, analysis of the replies which petitioners actually received showed a larger proportion of them to be of an explanatory form than this criticism might suggest. Nonetheless, there is an important distinction between replies which are simply 'expanded' or 'explanatory' and ones which give the reason for the decision and/or specifically counter the inmate's submission by showing that each point raised in the petition has been taken into consideration.

The importance attached by staff and inmates alike to having detailed replies to petitions, suggests that they make an important contribution to maintaining confidence in grievance procedures. Consideration should therefore be given to the scope for providing more detailed replies, despite the fact that this may have implications for resources.

The analysis of petitioners' files also showed them to contain much useful material about inmates' requests and grievances and of problems and pressures in the prison system. Some of this is monitored already by Prison Department, but more regular and systematic monitoring would enable more account to be taken of this information in policy formulation.

Appendix A: Population characteristics of the six prisons

i. Length of sentence being served

Prison	Percentage of sample								Number in sample
	Less than 6 months	6–11 months	12–23 months	24–47 months	4 years but less than 10 years	10 years but less than 15 years	15 years and over	Life	
Local 1	45	23	10	12	10	—	—	—	69
Local 2	35	19	19	17	10	—	—	—	48
Training 1	—	—	—	16	53	16	4	12	51
Training 2	11	—	7	39	34	2	—	7	44
Dispersal 1	—	—	—	—	58	16	4	22	50
Dispersal 2	—	—	—	—	47	13	11	29	55

ii. Length of time at current prison

Prison	Percentage of sample						Number in sample
	Less than 1 month	1 month but less than 3 months	3 months but less than 6 months	6 months but less than 1 year	1 year but less than 2 years	2 years or more	
Local 1	55	28	13	3	1	—	69
Local 2	54	35	6	2	2	—	48
Training 1	14	14	22	20	24	8	51
Training 2	14	23	27	25	7	5	44
Dispersal 1	6	28	22	28	12	4	50
Dispersal 2	13	7	11	18	25	25	55

iii. Offences for which convicted by offence group

Prison	Percentage of sample					Number in sample
	Violence	Sexual offences	Burglary and Robbery	Theft	Other	
Local 1	22	7	32	23	16	69
Local 2	10	—	38	31	21	48
Training 1	39	27	27	4	2	51
Training 2	39	2	27	18	14	44
Dispersal 1	40	4	42	4	10	50
Dispersal 2	42	5	38	5	9	55

iv. Age of inmates, by age group

Prison	Percentage of sample					Number in sample
	21–24	25–29	30–34	35–39	40 and over	
Local 1	45	23	12	7	13	69
Local 2	31	25	8	19	17	48
Training 1	18	24	12	16	31	51
Training 2	34	18	20	16	11	44
Dispersal 1	2	28	26	22	22	50
Dispersal 2	7	25	31	16	20	55

Appendix B: Entries in a wing application book

(Names and numbers removed)

WEDNESDAY 3 NOVEMBER 1982

Nature of application	Decision
Special letter to probation officer	Issued
Special letter to probation officer	Issued
Special letter to probation officer	Issued
Special children's letter	Issued
To have radio into possession	F35 to reception
To have photographs from property	F35 to reception
To see Governor for permission to 'dine out' (in association)	F32 to Chief Officer's Clerk
Special letter to probation officer	Issued
To see Governor to ask for a transfer	F35 to Chief Officer's Clerk
Special letter to solicitor	Issued
Permission to have extended visit	Entry to be made in Visits Book
To have a model handed in during visits	Entry to be made in Visits Book
To see Governor ref transfer	F35 to Chief Officer's Clerk
Special letter to probation officer	Issued
Permission to dine out (in association)	F35 to Chief Officer's Clerk
To hand out a radio on a visit	F35 to reception and enter Visits Book
To have canteen letters from property	F35 to reception

References

Home Office (1979). *Committee of Inquiry into the United Kingdom Prison Services (the 'May Report')*. London: HMSO.

Home Office (1980). *The Reduction of Pressure on the Prison System: observations on the fifteenth report of the Expenditure Committee*. London: HMSO.

House of Commons (1975). *First Report from the Select Committee on the Parliamentary Commissioner for Administration*. London: HMSO.

House of Commons (1978). *Fifteenth Report from the Expenditure Committee: the reduction of pressure on the prison system*. London: HMSO.

House of Commons (1981). *Fourth Report from the Home Affairs Committee: the prison service*. London: HMSO.

Justice (1983). *Justice in Prison: report of a Committee under the Chairmanship of Sir Brian MacKenna*. London: Justice.

Lawton, J. (1977). *Applications to Governors and Boards of Visitors at Preston and Haverigg*. Pilot study undertaken by the Home Office Research Unit. Unpublished.

Maguire, M. and Vagg, J. (1984). *The 'Watchdog' Role of Boards of Visitors*. London: Home Office.

Martin, J. P. (1975). *Boards of Visitors of Penal Institutions (the 'Jellicoe Committee')*. Chichester: Barry Rose.

Publications

Titles already published for the Home Office

Studies in the Causes of Delinquency and the Treatment of Offenders (SCDTO)

1. Prediction methods in relation to borstal training. Hermann Mannheim and Leslie T. Wilkins, 1955 viii + 276pp. (11 340051 9).

2. *Time spent awaiting trial. Evelyn Gibson. 1960. v + 45pp. (34-368-2).

3. Delinquent generations. Leslie T. Wilkins. 1960. iv + 20pp. (11 340053 5).

4. *Murder. Evelyn Gibson and S. Klein. 1961. iv + 44pp. (11 340054 3).

5. Persistent criminals. A study of all offenders liable to preventive detention in 1956. W. H. Hammond and Edna Chayen. 1963. ix + 237pp. (34-368-5).

6. *Some statistical and other numerical techniques for classifying individuals. P. McNaughton-Smith. 1965. v + 33pp. (34-368-6).

7. Probation research: a preliminary report. Part I. General outline of research. Part II. Study of Middlesex probation area (SOMPA). Steven Folkard, Kate Lyon, Margaret M. Carver and Erica O'Leary. 1966. vi + 58pp. (11 340374 7).

8. *Probation research: national study of probation. Trends and regional comparisons in probation (England and Wales). Hugh Barr and Erica O'Leary. 1966. vii + 51pp. (34-368-8).

9. *Probation research. A survey of group work in the probation service. Hugh Barr. 1966. vii + 94pp. (34-368-9).

10. *Types of delinquency and home background. A validation study of Hewitt and Jenkins' hypothesis. Elizabeth Field. 1967. vi + 21pp. (34-368-10).

11. *Studies of female offenders. No 1—Girls of 16–20 years sentenced to borstal or detention centre training in 1963. No 2—Women offenders in the Metropolitan Police District in March and April 1957. No 3—A description of women in prison on January 1, 1965. Nancy Goodman and Jean Price. 1967. v + 78pp. (34-368-11).

12. *The use of the Jesness Inventory on a sample of British probationers. Martin Davies. 1967. iv + 20pp. (34-368-12).

13. *The Jesness Inventory: application to approved school boys. Joy Moit. 1969. iv + 27pp. (11 340063 2).

Home Office Research Studies (HORS)

1. *Workloads in children's departments. Eleanor Grey. 1969. vi + 75pp. (11 340101 9).

2. *Probationers in their social environment. A study of male probationers aged 17–20, together with an analysis of those reconvicted within twelve months. Martin Davies. 1969. vii + 204pp. (11 340102 7).

3. *Murder 1957 to 1968. A Home Office Statistical Divison report on murder in England and Wales. Evelyn Gibson and S. Klein (with annex by the Scottish Home and Health Department on murder in Scotland). 1969. vi + 94pp. (11 340103 5).

4. Firearms in crime. A Home Office Statistical Division report on indictable offences involving firearms in England and Wales. A. D. Weatherhead and B. M. Robinson. 1970. vii + 39pp. (11 340104 3).

5. *Financial penalties and probation. Martin Davies. 1970. vii + 39pp. (11 3240105 1).

* Out of print.

6. *Hostels for probationers. A study of the aims, working and variations in effectiveness of male probation hostels with special reference to the influence of the environment on delinquency. Ian Sinclair. 1971. ix + 200pp. (11 340106 X).

7. *Prediction methods in criminology—including a prediction study of young men on probation. Frances H. Simon. 1971. xi + 234pp. (11 340107 8).

8. *Study of the juvenile liaison scheme in West Ham 1961–65. Marilyn Taylor. 1971. vi + 46pp. (11 340108 6).

9. *Exploration in after-care. I—After-care units in London, Liverpool and Manchester. Martin Silberman (Royal London Prisoners' Aid Society) and Brenda Chapman. II—After-care hostels receiving a Home Office grant. Ian Sinclair and David Snow (HORU). III—St. Martin of Tours House, Ayreh Leissner (National Bureau for Co-operation in Child Care). 1971. xi + 140pp. (11 340109 4).

10. A survey of adoption in Great Britain. Eleanor Grey in collaboration with Ronald M. Blunden. 1971. ix + 168pp. (11 340110 8).

11. *Thirteen-year-old approved school boys in 1962. Elizabeth Field, W. H. Hammond and J. Tizard. 1971. xi + 46pp. (11 34011 6).

12. Absconding from approved schools. R. V. G. Clarke and D. N. Martin. 1971. vi + 146pp. (11 340112 4).

13. An experiment in personality assessment of young men remanded in custody. H. Sylvia Anthony. 1972. viii + 79pp. (11 340113 2).

14. *Girl offenders aged 17–20 years. I—Statistics relating to girl offenders aged 17–20 years from 1960 to 1970. II—Re-offending by girls released from borstal or detention centre training. III—The problems of girls released from borstal training during their period on after-care. Jean Davies and Nancy Goodman. 1972. v + 77pp. (11 340114 0).

15. *The controlled trial in institutional research—paradigm or pitfall for penal evaluators? R. V. G. Clarke and D. B. Cornish. 1972. v + 33pp. (11 340115 9).

16. *A survey of fine enforcement. Paul Softley. 1973. v + 65pp. (11 340116 7).

17. *An index of social environment—designed for use in social work research. Martin Davies. 1973. vi + 63pp. (11 340117 5).

18. *Social enquiry reports and the probation service. Martin Davies and Andrea Knopt. 1973. v + 49pp. (11 340118 3).

19. *Depression, psychopathic personality and attempted suicide in a borstal sample. H. Sylvia Anthony. 1973. viii + 44pp. (0 11 340119 1).

20. *The use of bail and custody by London magistrates' courts before and after the Criminal Justice Act 1967. Frances Simon and Mollie Wetheritt. 1974. vi + 78pp. (0 11 340120 5).

21. Social work in the environment. A study of one aspect of probation practice. Martin Davies, with Margaret Rayfield. Alaster Calder and Tony Fowles. 1974. ix + 151pp. (0 11 340121 3).

22. Social work in prison. An experiment in the use of extended contact with offenders. Margaret Shaw. vii + 154pp. (0 11 340122 1).

23. Delinquency amongst opiate users. Joy Mott and Marilyn Taylor. vi + 31pp. (01 340663 0).

24. IMPACT. Intensive matched probation and after-care treatment. Vol. I—The design of the probation experiment and an interim evaluation. M. S. Folkard, A. J. Fowles, B. C. McWilliams, W. McWilliams. D. D. Smith, D. E. Smith and G. R. Walmsley. 1974. v + 54pp. (0 11 340664 9).

25. The approved school experience. An account of boys' experiences of training under differing regimes of approved schools, with an attempt to evaluate the effectiveness of that training. Anne B. Dunlop. 1974. vii + 124pp. (0 11 340665 7).

26. *Absconding from open prisons. Charlotte Banks, Patricia Mayhew and R. J. Sapsford. 1975. viii + 89pp. (0 11 340666 5).

27. Driving while disqualified. Sue Kriefman. 1975. vi + 136pp. (0 11 340667 3).

28. Some male offenders' problems. I—Homeless offenders in Liverpool. W. McWilliams. II—Casework with short-term prisoners. Julie Holborn. 1975. x + 147pp. (0 11 340668 1).

---

* Out of print.

29. *Community service orders. K. Pease, P. Durkin, I. Earnshaw, D. Payne and J. Thorpe. 1975. viii + 80pp. (0 11 340669 X).

30. Field Wing Bail Hostel: the first nine months. Frances Simon and Sheena Wilson. 1975. viii + 55pp. (0 11 340670 3).

31. Homicide in England and Wales 1967–1971. Evelyn Gibson. 1975. iv + 59pp. (0 11 340753 X).

32. Residential treatment and its effects on delinquency. D. B. Cornish and R. V. G. Clarke. 1975. vi + 74pp. (0 11 340672 X).

33. Further studies of female offenders. Part A: Borstal girls eight years after release. Nancy Goodman, Elizabeth Maloney and Jean Davies. Part B: The sentencing of women at the London Higher Courts. Nancy Goodman, Paul Durkin and Janet Halton. Part C: Girls appearing before a juvenile court. Jean Davies. 1976. vi + 114pp. (0 11 340673 8).

34. *Crime as opportunity. P. Mayhew, R. V. G. Clarke, A. Sturman and J. M. Hough. 1976. vii + 36pp. (0 11 340674 6).

35. The effectiveness of sentencing: a review of the literature. S. R. Brody. 1976. v + 89pp. (0 11 340675 4).

36. IMPACT. Intensive matched probation and after-care treatment. Vol II—The results of the experiment. M. S. Folkard, D. E. Smith and D. D. 1976. xi + 400pp. (0 11 340676 2).

37. Police cautioning in England and Wales. J. A. Ditchfield. 1976. v + 31pp. (0 11 340677 2).

38. Parole in England and Wales. C. P. Nuttall, with E. E. Barnard, A. J. Fowles, A. Frost, W. H. Hammond, P. Mayhew, K. Pease, R. Tarling and M. J. Weatheritt. 1977. vi + 90pp. (0 11 340678 9).

39. Community service assessed in 1976. K. Pease, S. Billingham and I. Earnshaw. 1977. vi + 29pp. (0 11 340679 7).

40. Screen violence and film censorship: a review of research. Stephen Brody. 1977. vii + 179pp. (0 11 340680 0).

41. Absconding from borstals. Gloria K. Laycock. 1977. v + 82pp. (0 11 340681 9).

42. Gambling: a review of the literature and its implications for policy and research. D. B. Cornish. 1978. xii + 284pp. (0 11 340682 7).

43. Compensation orders in magistrates' courts. Paul Softley. 1978. v + 41pp. (0 11 340683 5).

44. Research in criminal justice. John Croft. 1978. iv + 16pp. (0 11 340684 3).

45. Prison welfare: an account of an experiment at Liverpool. A. J. Fowles. 1978. v + 34pp. (0 11 340685 1).

46. Fines in magistrates' courts. Paul Softley. 1978. v + 42pp. (0 11 340686 X).

47. Tackling vandalism. R. V. G. Clarke (editor), F. J. Gladstone, A. Sturman and Sheena Wilson (contributors). 1978. vi + 91pp. (0 11 340687 8).

48. Social inquiry reports: a survey. Jennifer Thorpe. 1979. vi + 55pp. (0 11 340688 6).

49. Crime in public view. P. Mayhew, R. V. G. Clarke, J. N. Burrows, J. M. Hough and S. W. C. Winchester. 1979. v + 36pp. (0 11 340689 4).

50. *Crime and the community. John Croft. 1979. v + 16pp. (0 11 340690 8).

51. Life-sentence prisoners. David Smith (editor), Christopher Brown, Joan Worth, Roger Sapsford and Charlotte Banks (contributors). 1979. iv + 51pp. (0 11 340691 6).

52. Hostels for offenders. Jane E. Andrews, with an appendix by Bill Sheppard. 1979. v + 30pp. (0 11 340692 4).

53. Previous convictions, sentence and reconviction: a statistical study of a sample of 5,000 offenders convicted in January 1971. G. J. O. Phillpotts and L. B. Lancucki. 1979. v + 55pp. (0 11 340693 2).

54. Sexual offences, consent and sentencing. Roy Walmsley and Karen White. 1979. vi + 77pp. (0 11 340694 0).

55. Crime prevention and the police. John Burrows, Paul Ekblom and Kevin Heal. 1979. v + 37pp. (0 11 340695 9).

---

* Out of print.

75

56. Sentencing practice in magistrates' courts. Roger Tarling, with the assistance of Mollie Weatheritt. 1979. vii + 54pp. (0 11 340696).

57. Crime and comparative research. John Croft. 1979. iv + 16pp. (0 11 340697 5).

58. Race, crime and arrests. Philip Stevens and Carole F. Willis. 1979. v + 69pp. (0 11 340698 3).

59. Research and criminal policy. John Croft. 1980. iv + 14pp. (0 11 340699 1).

60. Junior attendance centres. Anne B. Dunlop. 1980. v + 47pp. (0 11 340770 9).

61. Police interrogation: an observational study in four police stations. Paul Softley, with the assistance of David Brown, Bob Forde, George Mair and David Moxon. 1980. vii + 67pp. (0 11 340701 7).

62. Co-ordinating crime prevention efforts. F. J. Gladstone. 1980. v + 74pp. (0 11 340702 5).

63. Crime prevention publicity: an assessment. D. Riley and P. Mayhew. 1980. v + 47pp. (0 11 340703 3).

64. Taking offenders out of circulation. Stephen Brody and Roger Tarling. 1980. v + 46pp. (0 11 340704 1).

65. *Alcoholism and social policy: are we on the right lines? Mary Tuck. 1980. v + 30pp. (0 11 340705 X).

66. Persistent petty offenders. Suzan Fairhead. 1981. vi + 78pp. (0 11 340706 8).

67. Crime control and the police. Pauline Morris and Kevin Heal. 1981. v + 71pp. (0 11 340707 6).

68. Ethnic minorities in Britain: a study of trends in their positions since 1961. Simon Field, George Mair, Tom Rees and Philip Stevens. 1981. v + 48pp. (0 11 340708 4).

69. Managing criminological research. John Croft. 1981. iv + 17pp. (0 11 340709 2).

70. Ethnic minorities, crime and policing: a survey of the experiences of West Indians and whites. Mary Tuck and Peter Southgate. 1981. iv + 50pp. (0 11 3240765 3).

71. Contested trials in magistrates' courts. Julie Vennard. 1982. v + 32pp. (0 11 340766 1).

72. Public disorder: a review of research and a study in one inner city area. Simon Field and Peter Southgate. 1982. v + 77pp. (0 11 340767 X).

73. Clearing up crime. John Burrows and Roger Tarling. 1982. vii + 31pp. (0 11 340768 8).

74. Residential burglary: the limits of prevention. Stuart Winchester and Hilary Jackson. 1982. v + 47pp. (0 11 340769 6).

75. Concerning crime. John Croft. 1982. iv + 16pp. (0 11 340770 X).

76. The British Crime Survey: first report. Mike Hough and Pat Mayhew. 1983. v + 62pp. (0 11 340789 6).

77. Contacts between police and public: findings from the British Crime Survey. Peter Southgate and Paul Ekblom. 1984. v + 42pp. (0 11 340771 8).

78. Fear of crime in England and Wales. Michael Maxfield. 1984. v + 51pp. (0 11 340772 6).

79. Crime and police effectiveness. Ronald V. Clarke and Mike Hough. 1984. iv + 33pp. (0 11 340773 4).

80. The attitudes of ethnic minorities. Simon Field. 1984. v + 50pp. (0 11 340774 2).

81. Victims of crime: the dimensions of risk. Michael Gottfredson. 1984. v + 54pp. (0 11 3240775 0).

82. The tape recording of police interviews with suspects: an interim report. Carole Willis. 1984. v + 45pp. (0 11 340776 9).

83. Parental supervision and juvenile delinquency. David Riley and Margaret Shaw. 1985. v + 90pp. (0 11 340799 8).

84. Adult prisons and prisoners in England and Wales 1970–82: a review of the findings of social research. Joy Mott. 1985. vi + 73pp. (0 11 340801 3).

85. Taking account of crime: key findings from the 1984 British Crime Survey. Mike Hough and Pat Mayhew. 1985. vi + 115pp. (0 11 340810 2).

86. Implementing crime prevention measures. Tim Hope. 1985. vi + 82pp. (0 11 340812 9).

87. Resettling refugees: the lessons of research. Simon Field. 1985. vi + 62pp. (0 11 340815 3).

---

* Out of print.

88. Investigating Burglary: the measurement of police performance. John Burrows. 1986.
    v + 36pp. (0 11 340824 2).
89. Personal violence. Roy Walmsley. 1986. vi + 87pp. (0 11 340827 7).
90. Police—public encounters. Peter Southgate with the assistance of Paul Ekblom. 1986.
    vi + 150pp. (0 11 340834 X).

ALSO

Designing out crime, R. V. G. Clarke and P. Mayhew (editors). 1980. vii + 186pp.
(0 11 340732 7.)

(This book collects, with an introduction, studies that were originally published in HORS
34, 47, 49, 55, 62 and 63 and which are illustrative of the 'situational' approach to crime
prevention.)

Policing today. Kevin Heal, Roger Tarling and John Burrows (editors). 1985. v + 181pp.
(0 11 340800 5.)

(This book brings together twelve separate studies on police matters produced during the last
few years by the Unit. The collection records some relatively little known contributions to
the debate on policing.)

Managing Criminal Justice: a collection of papers. David Moxon (editor). 1985. vi + 222pp.
(0 11 430811 0).

(This book brings together a number of studies bearing on the management of the criminal
justice system. It includes papers by social scientists and operational researchers working
within the Research and Planning Unit, and academic researchers who have studied
particular aspects of the criminal process.)

Situational Crime Prevention: from theory into practice. Kevin Heal and Gloria Laycock
(editors). 1986. vii + 166pp. (0 11 340826 9).

(Following the publication of Designing Out Crime, further research has been completed on
the theoretical background to crime prevention. In drawing this work together this book sets
down some of the theoretical concerns and discusses the emerging practical issues. It includes
contributions by Unit staff as well as academics from this country and abroad.)

The above HMSO publications can be purchased from Government Bookshops or through
booksellers.

The following Home Office research publications are available on request from the Home Office
Research and Planning Unit, 50 Queen Anne's Gate, London, SW1H 9AT.

Research Unit Papers (RUP)

1. Uniformed police work and management technology. J. M. Hough. 1980.
2. Supplementary information on sexual offences and sentencing. Roy Walmsley and Karen
   White. 1980.
3. Board of Visitor adjudications. David Smith, Claire Austin and John Ditchfield. 1981.
4. Day centres and probations. Suzan Fairhead, with the assistance of J. Wilkinson-Grey. 1981.

Research and Planning Unit Papers (RPUP)

5. Ethnic minorities and complaints against the police. Philip Stevens and Carole Willis. 1982.
6. *Crime and public housing. Mike Hough and Pat Mayhew (editors). 1982.
7. *Abstracts of race relations research. George Mair and Philip Stevens (editors). 1982.
8. Police probationer training in race relations. Peter Southgate. 1982.
9. *The police response to calls from the public. Paul Ekblom and Kevin Heal. 1982.
10. City centre crime: a situational approach to prevention. Malcolm Ramsay. 1982.
11. Burglary in schools: the prospects for prevention. Tim Hope. 1982.
12. *Fine enforcement. Paul Softley and David Moxon. 1982.
13. Vietnamese refugees. Peter Jones. 1982.

* Out of print.

14. Community resources for victims of crime. Karen Williams. 1983.
15. The use, effectiveness and impact of police stop and search powers. Carole Willis. 1983.
16. Acquittal rates. Sid Butler. 1983.
17. Criminal justice comparisons: the case of Scotland and England and Wales. Lorna J. F. Smith. 1983.
18. Time taken to deal with juveniles under criminal proceedings. Catherine Frankenburg and Roger Tarling. 1983.
19. Civilian review of complaints against the police: a survey of the United States literature. David C. Brown. 1983.
20. Police action on motoring offences. David Riley. 1983.
21. *Diverting drunks from the criminal justice system. Sue Kingsley and George Mair. 1983.
22. The staff resource implications of an independent prosecution system. Peter R. Jones. 1983.
23. Reducing the prison population: an explanatory study in Hampshire. David Smith, Bill Sheppard, George Mair and Karen Williams. 1984.
24. Criminal justice system model: magistrates' courts' sub-model. Susan Rice. 1984.
25. Measures of police effectiveness and efficiency. Ian Sinclair and Clive Miller. 1984.
26. Punishment practice by prison Boards of Visitors. Susan Iles, Adrienne Connors, Chris May, Joy Mott. 1984.
27. *Reparation, conciliation and mediation. Tony Marshall. 1984.
28. Magistrates domestic courts: new perspectives. Tony Marshall (editor). 1984.
29. Racism awareness training for the police. Peter Southgate. 1984.
30. Community constables: a study of policing initiative. David Brown and Susan Iles. 1985.
31. Recruiting volunteers. Hilary Jackson. 1985.
32. Juvenile sentencing: is there a tariff? David Moxon, Peter Jones and Roger Tarling. 1985.
33. Bringing people together: mediation and reparation projects in Great Britain. Tony Marshall and Martin Walpole. 1985.
34. Remands in the absence of the accused. Chris May. 1985.
35. Modelling the criminal justice system. Patricia M. Morgan. 1986.
36. The criminal justice system model: the flow model. Hugh Pullinger. 1986.
37. Burglary: police actions and victim views. John Burrows. 1986.
38. Unlocking community resources: four experimental government small grants schemes. Hilary Jackson. 1986.

Research Bulletin

The Research Bulletin is published twice a year and consists mainly of short articles relating to projects which are part of the Home Office Research and Planning Unit's research programme.

---

* Out of print.

Printed for Her Majesty's Stationery Office by Hobbs the Printers of Southampton
(2395/86) Dd239716 C13 9/86 G443